FAST TRACK

GENESIS TO REVELATION
The Quickest Way to Understand the Bible

CHAD HOVIND
Small-group experience written by Barry Cram

LifeWay Press®
Nashville, Tennessee

Fast Track
Genesis to Revelation: The Quickest Way to Understand the Bible
Published by LifeWay Press®
©2013 Chad Hovind

ISBN: 978-1-4158-7790-6
Item: 005558732

Dewey Decimal: 220.07
Subject Headings: BIBLE--STUDY \ DISCIPLESHIP \ BIBLE--CHRONOLOGY

Unless otherwise indicated, all Scripture quotations are taken from the Holman Christian Standard Bible®, Copyright © 1999, 2000, 2002, 2003 by Holman Bible Publishers. Used by permission.

Scriptures marked MSG are from The Message, copyright © 1993, 1994, 1995, 1996, 2001, 2002 by Eugene Peterson. Published by NavPress. Used by permission.

To order additional copies of this resource, order online at www.lifeway.com; write LifeWay Small Groups: One LifeWay Plaza, Nashville, TN 37234-0152; fax order to 615.251.5933; call toll-free 800.458.2772.

Adult Ministry Publishing
LifeWay Church Resources
One LifeWay Plaza
Nashville, TN 37234-0152

CONTENTS

ABOUT THE AUTHORS

CHAD HOVIND is an "edutainer" who makes the Bible come alive for all ages. With over 20 years of experience as a children's pastor, youth director, and lead teacher of a megachurch, Chad uses interactive teaching, impersonations, balloons, magic, juggling, science experiments, drama, and humor to show the relevance of the Bible to everyday life. He is the father of three kids and loves skiing, volleyball, soccer, and watching movies with his wife Beth.

Chad is the lead pastor of Horizon Community Church in Cincinnati, Ohio and speaks at men's conferences, marriage retreats, events, and creative workshops all over the country. He graduated from Moody Graduate School and Moody Bible Institute with degrees in television communications, pastoral ministries, and a Master of Arts in Ministry.

Chad is the author of *Godonomics, How to Save Our Country—and Protect Your Wallet—Through Biblical Principles of Finance* and *Fast Track*.

His teenagers call him a goofball, his wife calls him a dork, but he thinks of himself as Steve Martin meets Francis Schaeffer—only he's quick to admit that he's not as funny as Martin nor as smart as Schaeffer.

BARRY CRAM wrote the small-group experience for *Fast Track*. He considers himself a small-group conversationalist who loves to partner with churches across America. He has served as a lead writer and contributing writer for several small-group studies currently in print including *Stolen, Game Plan for Life*, and *Hosea to Malachi: Twelve Timeless Voices*. Barry thinks the ideal small-group space involves interacting with others through God's Word, listening for the Holy Spirit to teach us something through another person's story, and experiencing redemptive community. Barry and his wife Lisa live in the Dallas-Fort Worth area and love to get in on God's kingdom work.

◆ A WORD FROM CHAD ABOUT FAST TRACK

I learn best when I'm having fun. In the church today, there seems to be two equally bad alternatives: light and fluffy or dry and dusty. One is too shallow and one is too boring. The most important message in the universe should be communicated in a way that is deep, but compelling.

Many children and adults know Bible stories but don't know the Bible's larger *story*. They have lots of puzzle pieces but no place to fit all the stories together in a fun, memorable, and easy-to-remember way. For 20 years I looked for a way to give audiences a fun hook for the whole message of the Bible. I wanted them to understand the larger outline and framework for God's story in a way where all the biblical personalities and events could fall into place. The options I found were too long, too boring, or too complicated. Until *Fast Track* ...

Imagine a tool that is so easy that a 5-year-old can use it. Imagine a tool so fun a fifth grader is engaged in class and loves it. Imagine a style of teaching that allows everyone to draw while you teach—engaging them through sight, sound, and action.

Imagine a church filled with people of all ages who can pull out a napkin and explain the whole Bible using simple drawings and a tic-tac-toe grid. Imagine seekers, new believers, and mature Christ-followers feeling competent in knowing and applying the entire Bible.

The *Fast Track* method is so simple and memorable that it can be easily retaught in minutes. Now throw in laughter, action, and some aha moments as the entire church understands how the whole Bible points to Jesus. That is *Fast Track!*

We took thousands of people of all ages through *Fast Track* and were overwhelmed with reports from people from every age group who loved the lessons. *Fast Track* increases biblical understanding. And more importantly, it reveals Jesus—from Genesis to Revelation.

Chad Towne

HOW TO USE THIS STUDY

We're glad you've chosen to study *Fast Track*! As this study guides you through Genesis to Revelation, it is our prayer that you will not only develop a better understanding of God's Word but you will also begin to track along with the principle figures, major events, and thematic movements of Scripture. Before you get started, here is some helpful information about the different elements you'll encounter within the study.

Week Introduction

Each session begins with an overview of the week's topic. This material is designed to introduce you to the content you will study that week. Reading the introduction before your group meets will help you better understand the topic and the context for your time together.

Back Track

This time is designed to provide you with an opportunity to talk about what God has been revealing to you or what insights have resulted from your personal time during the week.

Framing the Story

This section provides a question or discussion starter designed to help you get familiar with the specific themes of the session and become comfortable with discussion.

Video Track

This section provides a grid for you to draw the icons (simple drawings that illustrate the stories) for each week as you watch Chad draw them on the video. The nine numbered items highlight some of the main teaching points from the video and can be used to process with your group what you heard and how you were affected. You may also want to use the bottom portion of the page to jot down important points from Chad's message that were particularly meaningful to you.

Group Track

This portion of your weekly group meeting will not only reinforce Chad's message, but also take you a little deeper into the truth of the Scriptures you are studying and give you an opportunity to integrate these truths into your own life.

Wrap

This section serves as a conclusion to the group time and summarizes key points from your small-group meeting each week. During this time you will also watch a short closing video message from Chad and have a few minutes to process that with your group.

Personal Track

These pages following each small-group session are intended to give you an opportunity to take what you've learned during the session and go a little deeper in private devotional settings with God. During your next group meeting you will have time to share some of what you've learned with your group.

Note: If your children are using the kid's edition of *Fast Track*, you will notice their materials utilize some different icons from the adult materials. This was done to communicate in terms and concepts the children can understand. We have included those icons on pages 188-189 of this book.

Know that as we prepared this study we were praying for you. It is our hope that God will truly bless you on your journey to better understand the greatest story ever told!

Fast Track

THE BEGINNING:
TRUST ME

GENESIS–EXODUS

GENESIS–EXODUS

"The best way to find out if you can
trust somebody is to trust them."
ERNEST HEMINGWAY

If a good relationship is based on honesty, and honesty is based on trust, which relationships in your life are strong and healthy? Which need some work or repair? Are any of your relationships suffering because of a lack of trust?

It would do us all good if we evaluated our friendships on a regular basis. Instead of reacting to a relationship gone wrong, we would be all the wiser to assess our relationships before they go wrong. We could see where communication could improve or which love language to use or when our actions inadvertently caused mistrust, strain, or fracture. Being proactive is always better than being reactive. We can build on what's important without suffering relational loss due to carelessness or inattention.

And what about our relationship with God? As we navigate through this broken world, there is a desire within us to lean on the Divine for comfort. Let this week's experience introduce you to the early accounts of God and humanity. Look at the trust factor between the Creator and His creation and understand how their relationship was shattered all because of a simple lack of trust. Watch how God deals with a self-trusting world and witness how humanity comes to terms with the new reality of good and evil.

BACK TRACK

Talk about the personal goals you have for this study. What do you hope to gain through learning about the power of God's grace from beginning to end—Genesis to Revelation?

FRAMING THE STORY

There are some traditional vocations that assume a public trust—banker, political leader, doctor, pastor. Think about famous individuals who have violated the public trust in the past. What did they do and how did your view of them change?

What are some natural responses or feelings associated with a lack of trust?

VIDEO TRACK

Genesis–Exodus

KEY POINTS

1. God created … and He said, "It is good."
2. God said, "Trust Me." But Adam and Eve didn't, and evil and death came into the world.
3. Noah trusted God. And God sent a rainbow and a promise. "I am reliable."
4. God provided a new world, but the people refused to enjoy it.
5. When Abram had totally given up, God showed up. And Abram trusted.
6. Jacob didn't want to wait on God. He took things into his own hands.
7. God was always with Joseph. "What you intended for evil, God intended for good."
8. God appeared to Moses in a burning bush. "I AM will go with you."
9. Those who trusted God were spared death. And a covenant relationship was formed.

NOTES

GROUP TRACK

Adam chose to disobey God even when he knew better.

Abraham was tired of waiting for God.

Isaac's family related to each other with jealousy and total dysfunction.

Jacob spent a lifetime trying to control others and manipulating his circumstances.

Moses spent much of his life avoiding his past.

How do you think these biblical characters would fit into our world today?

Which of these characters can you identify with most? Explain.

Based on the statements above, how do each of these case studies ultimately come back to this: "God, can I trust You?"

One of Jesus' most famous teachings is found in the Sermon on the Mount (Matthew 5–7). Jesus is beginning to teach about the kingdom of heaven, and He is introducing a new way to live with God. It's fresh and dynamic—different from the old, stale teaching of the religious leaders.

[25] This is why I tell you: Don't worry about your life, what
you will eat or what you will drink; or about your body,
what you will wear. Isn't life more than food and the body
more than clothing? [26] Look at the birds of the sky: They
don't sow or reap or gather into barns, yet your heavenly
Father feeds them. Aren't you worth more than they?
[27] Can any of you add a single cubit to his height by worrying?
[31] So don't worry, saying, "What will we eat?" or
"What will we drink?" or "What will we wear?" [32] For
the idolaters eagerly seek all these things, and your
heavenly Father knows that you need them.
MATTHEW 6:25-27,31-32

What do you think Jesus meant when He told them not to worry about their lives? How do you think His audience responded?

Much of Jesus' teaching is about everyday life and how we can trust God for even the smallest things.

Twice Jesus says, "Don't worry" and reassures us that we can trust God for daily provision. What other obstacles do you think contribute to a lack of trust in God in everyday life?

God doesn't just know our needs, He knows *us*. And even in this knowledge, He loves and cares about us. Take a moment to discuss the implications of a God who knows us completely. How might being known at such an intimate level contribute to your capacity for trust?

It's one thing to trust God for bread. It's another thing to trust God in battle with so much on the line. When King David was embarking on a warpath against enemy nations, it was customary to stop by the sanctuary, acknowledge his trust in God, and pray. In Psalm 20, David says,

> ⁶ Now I know that the LORD gives victory to His anointed;
> He will answer him from His holy heaven
> with mighty victories from His right hand.
> ⁷ Some take pride in chariots, and others in horses,
> but we take pride in the name of Yahweh our God.
> PSALM 20:6-7

What are the "chariots" and "horses" of our time? Describe the temptation to put your trust in those things before God.

When was the last time you felt compelled to trust God for something big in your life? How was that different from trusting Him for the little things in life?

Reread Psalm 20:6-7 above. Talk about specific reasons you have for believing this is true.

WRAP

The overarching theme of this week's study is that God isn't just viable, He's reliable. He is trustworthy and He proves this over and over in Scripture as we've already seen in just the first two books of the Bible.

We've also seen that even folks like Abraham, Moses, Adam, and Eve struggled with trusting God. It's not uncommon even with proclaiming believers.

Trusting God means yielding to His wisdom instead of our own.

> [5] Trust in the LORD with all your heart,
> and do not rely on your own understanding;
> [6] think about Him in all your ways,
> and He will guide you on the right paths.
> PROVERBS 3:5-6

In all we do, we need to pause and ask God for His wisdom as we learn to trust Him more.

Do you ever have trouble trusting God? In his video message, Chad challenges us to identify one area of our lives where we would be willing to trust God as reliable this week. Challenge yourself to step out and begin acting like He is reliable, even in the midst of your doubts. And watch how God uses your actions to transform you in that area.

God, help us to see when we are veering off of Your path. Remind us of the dead end that's coming when we choose to place our trust in ourselves instead of You. Give us the wisdom we need to get back on the trust path with You. Grant us the courage to trust You with the big things and the temperament to trust You with the little things, too. Amen.

PERSONAL TRACK

THE GARDEN

In the beginning, God did not sin-proof the garden of Eden. Why?

God could have not had the forbidden fruit (with all the knowledge of good and evil) so easily accessible. Parents child-proof their homes—locking low-level cabinets, tamper-proofing the doorknobs, gating off the stairs, covering hearth and coffee table corners with padding. Good parents keep their children as safe as possible.

God could have taken away our ability to freely choose. Parents limit their children's choices—menu selection, movie selection, bedtime, naptime, and mealtime. All good parents limit the choices of their children until they are old enough to make good decisions on their own.

Therein lies the answer to the above question. If God had sin-proofed the garden, that would have communicated mistrust.

If you ask a professional counselor, he or she would agree that mutual trust is the cornerstone for a healthy relationship. It is no different in our relationship with God. There has always been a mutual trust between God and mankind. He gave Adam and Eve an enormous amount of power and authority over their own lives. He trusted them to do what was right. And He trusts us to do the same. God has always trusted us.

When we break that trust, God pursues us and makes provision to keep us in a relationship with Him. We see this right after the first time Adam and Eve broke the trust and sinned against God. What was God's immediate reaction? How did He respond? He pursued them with a piercing question. "The LORD God called out to the man and said to him, 'Where are you?'" (Genesis 3:9).

> How have you experienced God pursuing you even when your relationship with Him wasn't the best?

God pursues us because He is good. Everything about Him is perfect. And He knows good when He sees it:

³ God said, "Let there be light," and there was light.
⁴ God saw that the light was good, and God separated
the light from the darkness. ⁵ God called the light
"day," and He called the darkness "night."
GENESIS 1:3-5

¹⁵ The LORD God took the man and placed him in the
garden of Eden to work it and watch over it. ¹⁸ Then
the LORD God said, "It is not good for the man to be
alone. I will make a helper as his complement."
GENESIS 2:15,18

⁶ God said, "Let there be an expanse between the waters,
separating water from water." ²⁷ So God created man in His own
image; ³¹ God saw all that He had made, and it was very good.
GENESIS 1:6,27,31

"It's good, it's not good, it's very good." Perfect discernment and full of goodness. We see a God who is not only perfect in judgment, but His knowledge moves Him to act on our behalf. God saw it wasn't good that Adam was alone and He did something about it. Then when Adam and Eve chose not to trust God anymore, He still pursued them. Motivated by love and guided by goodness, God is trustworthy and has our good in mind.

How do you need to work on your end of the mutual trust relationship you have with God?

What actions or attitudes do you need to change to show that you are trustworthy?

God, take me back to where we began our journey together. I want to be reminded of how awesome You are! Amen.

BABEL

As we continue to read the biblical account of early civilization, we can start to see a pattern of behavior developing. When Adam and Eve sinned and were separated from God, "The LORD God sent him away from the garden of Eden to work the ground from which he was taken. He drove man out" (Genesis 3:23-24). When Cain killed his brother Abel, the Scripture records that "Cain went out from the LORD's presence and lived in the land of Nod, east of Eden" (Genesis 4:16). A few generations later, Cain's family began doing what they wanted—marrying two wives instead of one (Genesis 4:19) and killing innocent men and claiming self-defense (Genesis 4:23-24).

Notice that it is at this time that people began to call upon the name of the Lord (Genesis 4:26). Just a few generations removed from Eden and humanity was already feeling the desperation of their self-destruction. It is difficult to start trusting God when we are used to trusting ourselves. We have developed our own coping mechanisms, defensive postures, and survival skills to get through life.

> Think of a time when you felt far from God because you quit trusting Him. How did you cope?

> If you met someone today in a similar situation, what advice would you give to point him or her in the right direction based on your personal experience?

When we stop trusting God, we start trusting ourselves. When we start trusting ourselves, humanity begins to unravel at the speed of sin. When we choose to not pursue Him, our flesh will find other ways to receive physical pleasure, inner peace, and purpose for living. This is that old pattern of behavior that kicks in when we replace trust in God with trust in us.

You would think that a cataclysmic flood would purge the world of sin, but we find ourselves in the same pattern—trusting ourselves instead of God. Someone once said, "The problem with most self-made men is they tend to worship their creator."

This describes the condition of mankind at the Tower of Babel. Puffed-up and proud of self-achievement, this generation decided to build a tower to heaven to bring glory to themselves instead of God. The following exchange happened just before God confused their speech and scattered them across the earth.

> [1] At one time the whole earth had the same language and vocabulary. [2] As people migrated from the east, they found a valley in the land of Shinar and settled there. [3] They said to each other, "Come, let us make oven-fired bricks." They used brick for stone and asphalt for mortar. [4] And they said, "Come, let us build ourselves a city and a tower with its top in the sky. Let us make a name for ourselves; otherwise, we will be scattered over the face of the whole earth."
>
> GENESIS 11:1-4

A self-centered pattern of behavior can place many different kinds of obstacles or roadblocks between us and God. What obstacle or roadblock do you most commonly face?

How does it affect your ability to trust God?

What is the one thing you can do or change today that would help you develop the virtue of humility?

God, help me to trust You more. Show me how and remind me to pursue humility. I do not want pride to get in the way of my relationship with You. Amen.

JACOB'S WRESTLING MATCH

In the world of leadership development, there's a school of thought that if a strength is overplayed, it will become a weakness. Have your strengths ever gotten in the way of your relationship with God? Explain.

In what ways have you developed your strengths to advance your place in life?

During the 1912 Summer Olympics, Martin Klein wrestled in a Greco-Roman Middleweight semi-final round that lasted 11 hours and 40 minutes. He won the match, but he was so tired afterward that he didn't have any energy left to compete in the final round. As a result, another wrestler advanced to the final round and won gold without having to compete against anyone. Klein had given it his everything; he just went all in at the wrong time. He couldn't finish strong and had to forfeit the gold.[1]

When we read the story of Jacob, we find someone who went all in with God. We see a man who wrestled God all night and would not let go until God blessed him.

> [24] Jacob was left alone, and a man wrestled with him until daybreak. [25] When the man saw that He could not defeat him, He struck Jacob's hip socket as they wrestled and dislocated his hip. [26] Then He said to Jacob, "Let Me go, for it is daybreak." But Jacob said, "I will not let You go unless You bless me." [27] "What is your name?" the man asked." Jacob," he replied. [28] "Your name will no longer be Jacob," He said. "It will be Israel because you have struggled with God and with men and have prevailed."
> GENESIS 32:24-28

In this situation Jacob's "blessing" was to actually be used by God, and so God had to touch Jacob's leg and injure him. It was only after Jacob came to grips with God and ceased his struggling, realizing that he could not go on without Him, that he received God's blessing. But God was determined to use and bless Jacob on His terms, not Jacob's. Jacob engaged God with all the strength he had, but it was God who changed Jacob's name to *Israel*.

Our strengths, no matter how powerful they are, still need to be surrendered to God. We still need to be rescued by God, even if it means being rescued from ourselves. No matter how awesome and talented we are, we do not have the ability to bless ourselves like God can bless us. As you move forward in life, don't end up like the Olympian who couldn't finish strong. Engage God with everything you have, but allow Him to use you. Allow God to take and tame your strengths for Him.

In what ways are you aggressively cooperating with God to accomplish life?

Think about the areas of your life you are handling in your own power. How is that exposing you in the long run?

What are you trusting God to accomplish in your life totally apart from your own power and strength?

1. *http://www.britannica.com/olympics/reflections/article-277332.*

God, help me to rely upon Your strength, not mine. Show me where I am trusting in myself more than in You. Amen.

JOSEPH'S SECRET FOR TRUSTING GOD

Consider some of the literary tragedies of centuries past: Victor Hugo's *Les Misérables*, Shakespeare's *Richard III,* or *Romeo and Juliet.* What makes a tragedy a real tragedy?

That question is easy to answer if you have ever talked to the main character in a movie or shouted aloud at the big screen: "Don't go in there!" "Get the flashlight, you idiot!" "Don't run into the woods!"

You can yell those things because you know something they don't know. You have a different perspective. While you see things from a different angle, the characters within the tragedy remain in the dark. And isn't this the essence of all tragedies? It would be a miserable existence to witness evil and suffering without end or purpose. When we have access to good but choose never to trust and experience it, this is the *real* tragedy.

> You planned evil against me; God planned it for good to bring about the present result—the survival of many people.
> GENESIS 50:20

This is where Joseph turns the corner and truly escapes such a tragedy. For the first time since the beginning, we actually see someone other than God handle the knowledge of good and evil with God's perspective. This is what keeps the life of Joseph far from being a tragedy.

Can you sense the optimism in Joseph's voice? Can you hear the relief as he verbalizes with his mouth what he knows in his heart to be true about God?

In the beginning, we read that God is the only One who can perfectly discern what is good for our lives. He is the only One who can take the evil actions and intentions of the Enemy and make them work for our good. This doesn't just speak of God's sovereignty; this speaks of His goodness. He can't help it. If God gets His hands on it, it's going to be good.

We are able to trust God more when we acknowledge His goodness in our lives regardless of our circumstances. We are able to trust God more when we view the world the way He views the world. The greatest tragedy in our lives isn't the evil or suffering we experience. The greatest tragedy is when we refuse to give it over to God.

> Consider your life as a literary work. Will it end up a tragedy? Is there a past or present experience that you have refused to give to God? What would it take for you to respond like Joseph did?

> Take some time today to verbally affirm God's goodness in your life.

God, help me trust You beyond my own strength, power, and wisdom. Show me how to finish strong in life without neglecting You. Amen.

MOSES AND THE BURNING BUSH

When was the last time God interrupted your daily routine to get your attention?

> [28] On the day the LORD spoke to Moses in the land of Egypt, [29] He said to him, "I am Yahweh; tell Pharaoh king of Egypt everything I am telling you." [30] But Moses replied in the LORD's presence, "Since I am such a poor speaker, how will Pharaoh listen to me?"
>
> EXODUS 6:28-30

Think about this seismic shift for a moment. Moses has been living a very quiet and simple life in the desert as a shepherd for the past 40 years. Within a matter of moments, the conversation he is having with a little bush that has caught on fire has now turned into an argument. Moses doesn't know the journey ahead—the Red Sea, the 12 spies, the gripes of the people, the Ten Commandments, the miracles, the covenant God will make with him, and another 40 years wandering in the wilderness.

Moses has simply gone from telling sheep what to do to telling the Pharaoh what to do. And he's having a hard time adjusting.

Sometime this week, read about the ten plagues found in Exodus 7:1–12:30. Each plague was aimed at one of the Egyptian gods, to prove that there was only one true God. This was God's way of showing His people that He is still trustworthy.

What other gods do you depend on (status, appearance, approval of others, money, etc.)?

When God wants His people to trust Him, He will show them one step at a time. What does this say about God's attitude toward us when we don't trust Him? It says He is willing to meet us wherever we are on our journey with Him, as long as we are willing to move forward. God hasn't changed since Eden. He has always trusted, always pursued, always provided, always made a way for us to get back to Him.

The tenth plague was special for a couple of reasons. First, it was the only plague that required participation and obedience on the part of the nation of Israel. Second, this event became the reason for annual celebration for God's people for thousands of years to come.

> This day is to be a memorial for you, and you must celebrate it as a festival to the LORD. You are to celebrate it throughout your generations as a permanent statute.
>
> EXODUS 12:14

How has trusting God in the little things in life helped you trust Him in the big things, too?

Looking back on your journey, write about a situation in which God required you to participate and obey—in trust.

God, remind me of how trustworthy You are today. Give me a glimpse and help me find the path that leads me to You. Amen.

Fast Track

THE CONQUESTS: DON'T GIVE UP

EXODUS–1 SAMUEL

EXODUS–1 SAMUEL

"When you are going through hell, keep on going.
Never never never give up."
WINSTON CHURCHILL

Our problems are not bigger than God. Our families may forsake us. Our enemies may frighten us. Our circumstances may discourage us. Our employers may fire us. Our children may blame us. Our emotions may betray us. Our sin may entangle us. Our health may fail us. But our God has never given up on us. And so we don't give up on God.

In times of turmoil, we search for a soothing voice. We desire to find someone who can saturate our mind with clarity and calmness. We search for an anchor of truth that steadies the course. We need someone who can relieve our worried heart and bring life into a paralyzed will. When we give in to the deceptive instinct of trusting ourselves, the next step is deadly for sure. Human nature leads us to rely on our own power, wisdom, and experience. When we choose to give up on God, we forget His goodness, His power, and His sovereignty.

Let this week's experience in *Fast Track* reveal a God who continually initiates a relationship with His people. Witness a good God who pursues the people He so desperately wants to save. Learn from those who have lived life with and without God. Learn from their mistakes, their miscalculations, and their inaction. God doesn't give up on us.

God is bigger than our problems.

BACK TRACK

The personal track devotionals you read this past week likely provoked new thoughts about trusting God more. Which area related to trusting God has surfaced in your life that you feel you need to change (developing humility, not overplaying your strengths, remembering God's goodness, etc.)? Explain.

FRAMING THE STORY

There are lots of movies that inspire us to never give up. Below you will find some of them. Using movie(s) from this list or others that have touched you personally, discuss those that have inspired you and how.

Lord of the Rings
Coach Carter
Forrest Gump
Cinderella Man
Remember the Titans
Braveheart
Dead Poets Society
Marley and Me
Rudy
The Bucket List
The Pursuit of Happyness

VIDEO TRACK

Exodus–1 Samuel

KEY POINTS

1. We fall short. Though they gave up on God, He didn't give up on them.
2. They wandered. They grumbled. God still didn't give up. "Be strong and courageous, because I am with you."
3. God brought down the walls of Jericho. God welcomes, forgives, and draws near to anyone who will trust Him.
4. Joshua conquered the land. Joshua divided the land. "As for me and my house, we will serve the Lord."
5. "Stop running and return to Me." God relentlessly pursued His people.
6. Samson did what was right in his own eyes, but eventually chose to return. God restored his strength and allowed him to deliver his people.
7. Samuel grew up and helped people return to God.
8. Saul became king. He began his reign with grace and wisdom.
9. When the people wanted to head in two different directions, Saul merged them into a common confidence in God's deliverance.

NOTES

GROUP TRACK

In our own personal journey with God, the pendulum can swing back and forth. The following statements illustrate how these biblical characters experienced the ebb and flow of life with God:

Caleb resolved that if God is for us, who can really be against us?

Rahab believed God and did the right thing in the face of adversity.

Gideon struggled with believing God's plan for his life.

Naomi needed time for her faith in God to return.

Samson needed serious deliverance from self.

Joshua decided that his entire house was going to serve God.

> How do these statements resonate with the ebb and flow of your relationship with God?

> What do these statements reveal about the Personhood of God in the face of our humanity?

Gideon and Samson had very different responses to God. When God spoke the truth to Samson concerning his role and mission, Samson was motivated by his own lusts and decided to do things his own way (Exodus 16-17). When God spoke to Gideon about his role and mission, he had to be convinced over and over again. At first Samson's strength was unbelievable, but his life took a slow, spiraling descent toward weakness. On the other hand, Gideon's military bravery and prowess at the beginning was far from convincing, but he became a mighty man in battle. Interestingly enough, though, both men are mentioned in the Bible as men of faith.

³² What more can I say? Time is too short for me to tell about Gideon, Barak, Samson, Jephthah, David, Samuel, and the prophets, ³³ who by faith conquered kingdoms, administered justice, obtained promises, shut the mouths of lions, ³⁴ quenched the raging of fire, escaped the edge of the sword, gained strength after being weak, became mighty in battle, and put foreign armies to flight. ³⁹ All these were approved through their faith.

HEBREWS 11:32-34,39

Look at what God did through these individuals. How have you seen His work similarly today? What kind of person does He tend to use for His purposes?

How would it change your approach to life decisions, career, relationships, family, etc. if you could see yourself as God sees you?

¹⁴ The LORD turned to him and said, "Go in the strength you have and deliver Israel from the power of Midian. Am I not sending you?" ¹⁵ He said to Him, "Please, LORD, how can I deliver Israel? Look, my family is the weakest in Manasseh, and I am the youngest in my father's house." ¹⁶ "But I will be with you," the LORD said to him. "You will strike Midian down as if it were one man." ¹⁷ Then he said to Him, "If I have found favor in Your sight, give me a sign that You are speaking with me. ¹⁸ Please do not leave this place until I return to You. Let me bring my gift and set it before You." And He said, "I will stay until you return."

JUDGES 6:14-18

The story of Gideon strikes close to home. He reminds us of what Paul says to the Corinthians: "When I am weak, then I am strong" (2 Corinthians 12:10). Gideon's faith may have been weak, but it was enough faith to fulfill God's plans. And as time went on, he gathered both courage and faith.

Put yourself in Gideon's shoes for a minute. God has just told you to, "Go in the strength you have" and conquer those people who have been terrorizing you for generations. What are you thinking?

Who or what are your "Midianites" right now and what is the "strength you have"?

> If you have faith the size of a mustard seed, you will
> tell this mountain, "Move from here to there," and it
> will move. Nothing will be impossible for you.
> MATTHEW 17:20

Remember that faith can be very small—as small as a mustard seed. It is not the size of the seed that determines the ultimate outcome but the kind and quality of the seed. We can always use whatever small portion of faith we have to take the next step ... and the next ... and the next.

WRAP

There are so many ways to run from God. And we're all runners at one time or another, in one way or another. But our God is a God who comes after us when we run. And even when we give up on Him, He never gives up on us.

> The One who is in you is greater than the one who is in the world.
> 1 JOHN 4:4

What's one area of your life where you're running or rebelling? What would it take for you to stop running and return to Him?

Spend some time this week getting better acquainted with the God who runs after you. The God who desperately wants you to believe Him, stop running, return, and never give up again.

Never giving up means that we never disengage God. It doesn't matter how bad it gets, or how far we have run, or how empty we are, or how broken our relationship, or how helpless we feel. It doesn't matter! God is there for us. He will always be there for us. "I will never leave you or forsake you" (Hebrews 13:5). No matter how hard life gets, God is there with us.

And in surrendering to Him, we become more free, not less.

God, we pause to thank You for accepting us where we are on our spiritual journey. But thank You, too, for expecting us to grow along with You. While Your love unconditionally accepts us here, Your righteousness unapologetically propels us forward. Help us to engage our personal faith in You on a daily basis. Amen.

PERSONAL TRACK

FOLLOWER'S REMORSE

The *wilderness*. Just saying that word conjures up images of wide expenses of land with a whole lot of nothing. But after the Exodus, this is exactly where Moses found himself.

Exodus 12:37-38 tells us that Moses left Egypt on foot with 600,000 men and their families. With women and children, there may have been 2 million people plus. Imagine the burden of leading and feeding these people.

The trip was not supposed to be a long one. From Egypt it was about 250 miles to Canaan. This is about a 13-day trip. God didn't take the Israelites to Canaan directly, though. According to Exodus 13:17, God didn't want the Philistines to attack them, so He took them a different way through the wilderness. The original journey to the Promised Land took a little over two years.

But what a land it was! God had promised Moses from the burning bush that He would lead His people to a fertile land flowing with milk and honey. A blessed land for a blessed people. But since this land was already inhabited, God asked Moses to send in some men to scout it out—do a little recon. Moses chose one man from each of the 12 tribes and instructed them to return with information about the land and the people in it.

Two men, Joshua and Caleb, said, "let's go." Ten others said, "not so fast."

> They gave a negative report to the Israelites about the land they had scouted: "The land we passed through to explore is one that devours its inhabitants, and all the people we saw in it are men of great size."
> NUMBERS 13:32

> [1] The whole community broke into loud cries, and the people wept that night. [2] All the Israelites complained about Moses and Aaron, and the whole community told them, "If only we had died in the land of Egypt, or if only we had died in this wilderness! [3] Why is the LORD bringing us into this land to die by the sword? Our wives and little children will become plunder. Wouldn't it be better for us to go back to Egypt?" [4] So they said to one another, "Let's appoint a leader and go back to Egypt."
>
> NUMBERS 14:1-4

It seemed like no matter how many times God provided for the Israelites, they still found something about which they could complain. As a result, only Caleb and Joshua would be allowed to see the land because they had trusted God. As for the rest, God said that their bodies would fall in the desert after 40 years of wandering aimlessly in circles.

Why would God lead them all this way just to turn them back? The wilderness here seemed to be the best place for the faint of heart, for the lukewarm. In the wilderness character is built. In the wilderness we have a chance to trust God—not only in the good times but in the bad times, too.

In what ways have you viewed God like the people viewed Moses—with "follower's remorse"?

In another wilderness it was discovered that "man must not live on bread alone but on every word that comes from the mouth of God" (Matthew 4:4). Have you ever had a wilderness experience? How did God bless you and provide for you during this time?

God, I'm not giving up on You. I believe that You aren't done with me yet. Help me carry on and carry out Your plan for my life. Amen.

GOD LISTENS

"When to lead is as important as what to do and where to go.
Only the right action at the right time will bring success."
JOHN MAXWELL

Moses led God's people out of Egypt and to the Promised Land. It was a hard journey, but he got them there. Think about the 40 years of obstacles in their path as they walked through the desert toward what God had promised them. It took a courageous leader to not give up on God or His people. And even though Moses died outside the Promised Land, he never gave up the task of leading the people. Amazingly, Moses never forfeited his influence on the nation of Israel. This is the essence of endurance.

> Think about your role as a leader in the different areas of your life—work, family, or ministry. What steps are you taking to be the best leader you can be?

> Why is it important for a person with a sphere of influence to not give up on God?

Joshua would be the new leader for a new generation. He knew that they would have to take by force the land God had given them. He was charged by God from the start to be "strong and courageous" in everything that was before him, and he also led the people to be strong and courageous. God told him,

> [5] No one will be able to stand against you as long as you live. I will be with you, just as I was with Moses. I will not leave you or forsake you. [6] "Be strong and courageous, for you will distribute the land I swore to their fathers to give them as an inheritance. [7] Above all, be strong and very courageous to carefully observe the whole instruction My servant Moses

commanded you. Do not turn from it to the right or the left,
so that you will have success wherever you go. ⁹ Haven't I
commanded you: be strong and courageous? Do not be afraid or
discouraged, for the Lord your God is with you wherever you go."
JOSHUA 1:5-7,9

Joshua took God at His word. While battling his enemies, he actually prayed to God that the sun would stand still until they had victory. An unbelievable prayer that was answered by God.

¹² Joshua spoke to the Lord in the presence of Israel:
"Sun, stand still over Gibeon,
and moon, over the Valley of Aijalon."
¹³ And the sun stood still
and the moon stopped
until the nation took vengeance on its enemies.
Isn't this written in the Book of Jashar?
So the sun stopped
in the middle of the sky
and delayed its setting
almost a full day.
¹⁴ There has been no day like it before or since, when the Lord
listened to the voice of a man, because the Lord fought for Israel.
JOSHUA 10:12-14

What are you asking God to help you accomplish for Him? When He speaks to you, are you taking Him at His word?

God, help me stay in constant communion with You so that I can be the influential leader You intend for me to be. May I never take that responsibility lightly. Amen.

THE UNEXPECTED

You may have heard it said that it's not what you know but who you know that counts. Many people seem to get ahead in life due to knowing just the right person, being born into the right family, or by a chance encounter with someone. This is true of the spies sent by Joshua into the land of Jericho. They managed to gain entry, but their arrival did not go unnoticed. They had been seen and the king was told they were there. Imagine a chase scene through crowded city streets and a narrow escape with the spies finding themselves in the company of someone unexpected … a prostitute!

4 The woman had taken the two men and hidden them. So she said, "Yes, the men did come to me, but I didn't know where they were from. 5 At nightfall, when the gate was about to close, the men went out, and I don't know where they were going. Chase after them quickly, and you can catch up with them!" 6 But she had taken them up to the roof and hidden them among the stalks of flax that she had arranged on the roof. 7 The men pursued them along the road to the fords of the Jordan, and as soon as they left to pursue them, the gate was shut. 8 Before the men fell asleep, she went up on the roof 9 and said to them, "I know that the LORD has given you this land and that the terror of you has fallen on us, and everyone who lives in the land is panicking because of you. 10 For we have heard how the LORD dried up the waters of the Red Sea before you when you came out of Egypt, and what you did to Sihon and Og, the two Amorite kings you completely destroyed across the Jordan. 11 When we heard this, we lost heart, and everyone's courage failed because of you, for the LORD your God is God in heaven above and on earth below. 12 Now please swear to me by the LORD that you will also show kindness to my family, because I showed kindness to you. Give me a sure sign 13 that you will spare the lives of my father, mother, brothers, sisters, and all who belong to them, and save us from death."

JOSHUA 2:4-13

The men agreed. Within days, God's people moved out across the Jordan to advance on Jericho. The city fell, and Rahab and her family were spared. From that point onward, Rahab lived among the Israelite people. She married a man named Salmon.

They had a son named Boaz.

Boaz had a son named Obed.

Obed had a son named Jesse.

Jesse had a son named David.

Unexpected happenstance or divine providence?

Rahab recounted events that happened 40 years in the past. Take some time to think about how God has revealed Himself to you in the past. In what ways does that remind you of how powerful and good He really is?

Have you ever had an encounter with someone unexpected? How did it turn out?

What did you have in common with this person? How were you different?

God, let me live my life with the big picture in mind. Lead me to make the right decisions that will positively affect the future of my own family. Amen.

GIVE ME A SIGN

Batman, Spiderman, James Bond. There has been a huge increase in the last few years of superhero movies, and many have been blockbuster hits. *The Avengers* was so popular it brought in over 1.5 billion dollars in box office receipts worldwide.

> What do you think is the fascination with heroes/hero movies? Why do you think they are so popular in our culture?

In the Book of Judges we see stories of individuals who accomplished great things. Sometimes we think, *"That's heroic! That person is a hero!"* Maybe they didn't turn invisible, or fly in armored suits and battle aliens from another planet, or turn green and smash things and kill people with extraordinary strength. But there was one guy who did smash things and kill people with extraordinary strength. His name was Samson. He had great strength, and the angrier he became, the more damage he could do. Killing a lion with his bare hands, destroying an army with a donkey's jawbone, and pushing an entire pagan temple to the ground with his brute strength. This guy was truly unbelievable!

The Israelites were under God's judgment because they had stopped trusting Him. Their crops were being destroyed and their animals slaughtered by a persistent enemy from Midian. They cried out to God for help, attempting to break the cycle. And that's when another kind of hero emerged. His name was Gideon. He was the reluctant hero in waiting. He was the man who couldn't see his full potential. He was the hesitant hero who needed a sign. Actually, he needed *three* signs from God before he would move forward.

> [12] The Angel of the LORD appeared to him and said:
> "The LORD is with you, mighty warrior."
> [13] Gideon said to Him, "Please Sir, if the LORD is with us,
> why has all this happened? And where are all His wonders
> that our fathers told us about? They said, 'Hasn't

the LORD brought us out of Egypt?' But now the LORD has abandoned us and handed us over to Midian."
14 The LORD turned to him and said, "Go in the strength you have and deliver Israel from the power of Midian. Am I not sending you?"
15 He said to Him, "Please, Lord, how can I deliver Israel? Look, my family is the weakest in Manasseh, and I am the youngest in my father's house."
16 "But I will be with you," the LORD said to him. "You will strike Midian down as if it were one man."
17 Then he said to Him, "If I have found favor in Your sight, give me a sign that You are speaking with me."

JUDGES 6:12-17

Which do you think Gideon doubted more—God or himself? Explain.

At what point in your journey with God have you found yourself in Gideon's predicament? How do you get past self-doubt?

Who does God say you are? Are you willing to embrace that truth?

God, help me get beyond my doubt. Let me experience life in Your power and confidence, not mine. Help me believe who You say I am. Amen.

THE BEGINNING OF SOMETHING NEW

Think of your favorite NFL football team. What if the head coach refused to do the hard work and deliver wins? Even worse, what if the owner of the team hired his two sons to be offensive and defensive coaches and neither of them took their job seriously, losing every game?

This was the priest Eli and his two sons.

> [12] Eli's sons were wicked men; they had no regard for the LORD. [22] Now Eli was very old. He heard about everything his sons were doing to all Israel and how they were sleeping with the women who served at the entrance to the tent of meeting. [23] He said to them, "Why are you doing these things? I have heard about your evil actions from all these people. [24] No, my sons, the report I hear from the LORD's people is not good. [25] If a man sins against another man, God can intercede for him, but if a man sins against the LORD, who can intercede for him?" But they would not listen to their father, since the LORD intended to kill them. [26] By contrast, the boy Samuel grew in stature and in favor with the LORD and with men.
>
> 1 SAMUEL 2:12,22-26

This family of three had failed God in their spiritual leadership. Eli had given up on his boys, and his boys had given up on God. They refused to trust, obey, and follow Him. God reminded Eli, "I will honor those who honor Me, but those who despise Me will be disgraced" (1 Samuel 2:30). Soon God would bring judgment upon Eli by promising to cut off his household from the priestly line. His two sons, Hophni and Phinehas, would die on the same day. This would be the sign that God had brought judgment on them.

But God was already preparing another leader—a different kind of leader—who would listen to Him and lead His people. Samuel was only a boy at the time of his calling, but he would eventually lead the nation of Israel and speak on behalf of God for his entire life. The first of many prophets, Samuel set the standard for pro-claiming God's Word to the people, reminding them to follow God, and encouraging them to never give up.

> The boy Samuel served the LORD in Eli's presence.
> In those days the word of the LORD was rare and
> prophetic visions were not widespread.
> 1 SAMUEL 3:1

Let Eli & Co. represent the people or things that influence you away from God and let Samuel represent the people or things that influence you toward God. Who has the greater influence over you? Explain.

Do you need to make a change in your sphere of influence? Be specific.

God, help me to find and surround myself with the right people to influence my life toward You. Help me to be that influence to others, too. Amen.

Fast Track

THE MONARCHS: STOP RUNNING AND RETURN TO ME

1 SAMUEL–1 KINGS

1 SAMUEL–1 KINGS

> "Guitarist Brian 'Head' Welch ... has chosen
> Jesus Christ as his savior, and will be dedicating
> his musical pursuits to that end."
> STATEMENT FROM KORN, FEB 22, 2005 [1]

When we stop running from God, people notice. They notice because we are heading one way and then we change direction. In the I Am Second videos, different celebrities tell their stories. In almost every instance there's a point when you hear something like, "I stopped running from God," or "This is when I turned to God." It's part of every Christian's journey, no matter how far or how long we run. There's a course correction.

When Jesus taught that the Son of man must suffer and be killed, Peter argued with Jesus because he didn't fully understand His plan. Peter thought he was protecting Jesus. James and John argued over who would be the best in God's kingdom. They wanted honor and power for themselves.

The prostitute caught in the act heard these words from Jesus, "Where are your accusers?" Then the ever-so-important follow-up statement: "Go and sin no more." *Go and sin no more. Stop running and return to Me.* Same thing.

We get the best of both worlds when we stop and return to Him. This has been the message of God since the first days of disobedience. God's pursuit of Adam and Eve in the garden echoes throughout this week's session. We realize that God is not accusing us but has forgiven—and will continue to forgive—us. We also realize that we have a new path to travel, and this path brings us closer to God.

1. James Montgomery, "Brian 'Head' Welch Leaves Korn, Citing Moral Objections To Band's Music," MTV [online] 22 Feb. 2005 [cited 2 Mar. 2013]. Available from the Internet: *http://www.mtv.com/news/articles/1497313/brian-head-welch-leaves-korn.jhtml.*

BACK TRACK

Since your last group meeting, the personal study material had you focus on different aspects of never giving up. In what new ways has God inspired or challenged you to become a better leader or to move past self-doubt?

FRAMING THE STORY

Cary Grant, W. C. Fields, Peter Pan, and Annie. What do these celebrities have in common? They all ran away from home as kids or young teenagers. Running away from home has probably crossed the mind of every kid in America. Discuss the reasons why some kids want to run away.

VIDEO TRACK

1 Samuel–1 Kings

KEY POINTS

1. Saul became a broken ruler. His attention was on the wrong things.
2. Saul lost his faith, his family, his future.
3. Saul died in pain and agony, with relationships broken.
4. David was anointed as king. He had a heart for God.
5. David became complacent and started to give his attention to other things.
6. David lost his moral integrity and the effects caused cracks in the foundation of his family.
7. God offered Solomon a gift. Solomon asked for wisdom.
8. Solomon turned his attention to pleasure, status, beauty, and money. But his soul was unsatisfied by all the trappings of success, pleasure, and status.
9. Solomon's heart was divided. His kingdom was divided as well.

NOTES

GROUP TRACK

Saul, David, and Solomon. Each of these men rose to kingly power in different ways under different circumstances. Each had his weaknesses that contributed to a half-hearted devotion to God. Over time, Saul became jealous, David became complacent, and Solomon became hedonistic and bored. Each ran from God in his own way. These three kings are living examples of how difficult it is to remain disciplined and focused on following God.

How do each of these—jealousy, complacency, and boredom—play their own unique part as obstacles for those who are trying to follow God?

The Lord said: … These people approach Me with their mouths to honor Me with lip-service—yet their hearts are far from Me, and their worship consists of man-made rules learned by rote.
ISAIAH 29:13

This passage points to a difference between what we say and what we really believe. How do you think this distinction applies to us when we struggle to return to God?

What other issues—spiritual, cultural, emotional—tend to keep us from returning to God?

Jesus told many parables about the kingdom of God—His rules for living, His passion for us. Luke records three stories back-to-back that convey God's heart for those who need to return to Him. Here's a story about lost sheep.

[3] So He told them this parable: [4] "What man among you, who has
100 sheep and loses one of them, does not leave the 99 in the
open field and go after the lost one until he finds it?
[5] When he has found it, he joyfully puts it on his shoulders,
[6] and coming home, he calls his friends and neighbors
together, saying to them, "Rejoice with me, because I have
found my lost sheep!" [7] I tell you, in the same way, there will
be more joy in heaven over one sinner who repents than
over 99 righteous people who don't need repentance.

LUKE 15:3-7

Why do you think Jesus begins with a question like verse 4?

Look closely at verse 5. If Jesus was going to use you to claim this one lost
sheep, what would that require of you? Who is that sheep?

We deal with many issues—pride, self-reliance, lust, selfishness, you name it.
Anything can get between us and God. We need to keep watch, be diligent, and stay
vigilant in recognizing these issues. What does it take to get someone's attention so
they will stop and return to God? Hopefully it's our own relationship with God and
the conviction that follows when we stray away. The Proverbs are full of everyday,
practical warnings for those who follow God. Even though no one will ever be temp-
tation-free, there are ways to help us stay on the right path.

Keep vigilant watch over your heart;
that's where life starts.
Don't talk out of both sides of your mouth;
avoid careless banter, white lies, and gossip.

Keep your eyes straight ahead;
ignore all sideshow distractions.
Watch your step,
and the road will stretch out smooth before you.
Look neither right nor left;
leave evil in the dust.
PROVERBS 4:23-27, MSG

What "sideshow distractions" are most disruptive in your life?

What are the instructions attached to the warning to "keep vigilant watch over your heart"? What do they mean, and how are they related to this warning?

Let's get practical. Write down the one or two things that you could change right now that would help you to "ignore all sideshow distractions." If you need to, find some time this week to share with someone and solicit some accountability.

WRAP

Nobody wants to end their life in pain and devastation—like the kings we have studied this week. But the only way to ensure that doesn't happen and to make sure we are making wise choices is to ask for input.

How difficult is it for you to ask for input—from an employer, a family member, a friend, a trusted counselor, or pastor?

Consider what is on the line if you don't. David's situation is a great reminder that our choices and decisions don't just affect us. The ripple effect of the actions we take will impact everyone around us.

We don't always make wise choices. And many times we don't realize until afterward how much we've affected our own lives as well as the lives of those we care about. But if we return to God, He promises He will come to us in our brokenness and help us put our house back in order.

Nelson Mandela said, "There is nothing like returning to a place that remains unchanged to find the ways in which you yourself have altered." If you have found yourself wandering, return to God. It's comforting to know that even when we veer off course and change our minds or hearts, God hasn't moved. He does not change. God is the same yesterday, today, and forever.

We acknowledge our need for You, God. Help us to see where we took the wrong turn. God, give us a clear path back to You. We don't want to run anymore ... unless it's back into Your presence!

PERSONAL TRACK

SAUL

Have you ever witnessed someone's life unravel right before your eyes? Explain.

Athletes. Movie stars. Celebrities. The downward spiral is not fun to watch. You see the potential of what could have been completely vanish.

Self-reliance can sometimes be a virtue. But too much reliance on self can be disastrous. Sometimes it is a symptom of something deeper.

Can you remember the last time you truly felt alone? What did you do to get past this feeling?

Saul was the first king of Israel. He was appointed to leadership by Samuel, a prophet of God and the last judge of Israel, after the people saw that Samuel's sons were not fit for leadership.

The people cried out and argued with God for a king. So, God gave them Saul.

At first it seemed Saul would be the perfect leader.

God was the one who pointed out Saul to Samuel. The future king's appearance was impressive:

> He had a son named Saul, an impressive young man.
> There was no one more impressive among the Israelites
> than he. He stood a head taller than anyone else.
> 1 SAMUEL 9:2

Samuel asked Saul to have a meal with him and told him that he had been chosen to lead Israel. Samuel instructed him to go to Gilgal and wait seven days. Samuel would come and perform the sacrifice. After this, Samuel summoned all the people to present Saul as the new king, but Saul was nowhere to be found. Where was Saul? Was he being humble or running from his calling? Or was this just a foreshadowing of what was to come? King Saul was a jealous loner with rebellion hidden in his heart.

Later when Saul was in Gilgal and the Philistines were prepared to attack, his army was running off in fear. King Saul felt he couldn't wait for Samuel to come and make the sacrifice, so he took matters into his own hands and made the sacrifice himself even though he was not a priest. Rather than choosing to wait on God, he thought it best to do God's work his own way. God was already on the lookout for Saul's replacement.

> How do you think Saul felt at this point? He had just been made king.
> Why would God judge him so harshly over this one mistake?

It didn't get any better. God commanded Saul to destroy the Amalekites and all their belongings, but instead Saul kept everything that was good and destroyed the rest. At that point God regretted making Saul king and withdrew His Spirit from him. Even though he was still king, Saul was no longer blessed by God. Saul made a choice—to live his life his own way, apart from the commands of God. The cost was his sanity, his relationships, and eventually his life.

> What safeguards can you put in place to avoid going your own way against God?

Help me, God, to remain dependent on You. I don't want to be alone in this life.
If I am wandering, help me turn and run back to You. Amen.

ON THE RUN FOR GOOD

To what degree have you experienced personal jealousy? What do you think is the root cause of those feelings?

What things do you typically do to get past feeling this way?

The relationship between David and Saul was extremely complicated. By the time David arrived on the scene, both he and Saul knew that David would be the next king. Driving Saul even more into insanity was the fact that David was just a child. But he was a child who knew and followed God.

Consider this crazy analogy. A long-term, somewhat successful, extremely loyal CEO of a huge company is about to be replaced by a young, hotshot kid straight out of high school—not college, but high school. This was what King Saul experienced and it drove him mad!

> ¹⁴ Now the Spirit of the LORD had left Saul, and an evil spirit sent from the LORD began to torment him, ¹⁵ so Saul's servants said to him, "You see that an evil spirit from God is tormenting you. ¹⁶ Let our lord command your servants here in your presence to look for someone who knows how to play the lyre. Whenever the evil spirit from God troubles you, that person can play the lyre, and you will feel better."
> ¹⁹ Then Saul dispatched messengers to Jesse and said, "Send me your son David, who is with the sheep."
> ²¹ When David came to Saul and entered his service, Saul admired him greatly, and David became his armor-bearer. ²² Then Saul sent word to Jesse: "Let David remain in my service, for I am pleased with him." ²³ Whenever the spirit from God troubled Saul, David would pick up his lyre and play, and Saul would then be relieved, feel better, and the evil spirit would leave him.
> 1 SAMUEL 16:14-16,19,21-23

Saul had lost God's favor, and not too long afterward he lost the heart of the nation he was leading. After the little shepherd boy David defeated Goliath, he won the heart of the people of Israel. It was obvious that God was with David. Saul began to burn with jealousy. Not even the lyre could comfort him anymore. He tried twice in one day to kill David with a spear. Saul sent him into battles thinking the Philistines would defeat him, but David always emerged victorious.

For King Saul, there was no way to win. No matter what he did against David, David always came out on top. The people loved David. Even Saul's own son loved David. Saul's hatred burned so hot that David spent a few years hiding in caves, running for his life.

This was a dark time for David, but it forged a lifelong lesson in him. Gene Edwards, in *A Tale of Three Kings*, wrote, "David was caught in a very uncomfortable position; however, he seemed to grasp a deep understanding of the unfolding drama in which he had been caught. He seemed to understand something that few of even the wisest men of his day understood. ... And what was that? ... God wanted a broken vessel."[1]

David learned about personal brokenness, but he also learned of the goodness of God.

> When David was running *from* Saul, it taught him to run *to* God. What hard experiences in your life have taught you to run to God?

1. Gene Edwards, *A Tale of Three Kings* (Carol Stream, IL: Tyndale House Publishers, 1992), 12.

God, the contrast between Saul and David is stark. The choice is obvious. I don't want to be Saul. I want to be David. Help me to pursue You all the days of my life.

CONFRONTING THE KING

How would you feel if the worst thing you ever did became public knowledge? How would you react?

The Bible says David was a man after God's own heart, and he ruled his kingdom well. Up to the point where he became king, his story was picture perfect. He was bold and decisive, and he regularly inquired of the Lord's direction and wisdom. Surrounded by enemies, he waged countless battles and emerged victorious. He expanded Israel's territory, and the nation loved him. You would think he was on top of the world, that he could do no wrong.

Reading this story for the first time, it's hard to believe what happens next. David sleeps with Bathsheba, the wife of Uriah, a close, trusted friend and battle-worn warrior. This man had risked his life in battle for King David many times.

Once David finds out that Bathsheba is pregnant with his child, David tries to cover it up by bringing Uriah home from his military post. Surely he would come home to his wife and sleep with her. But Uriah refused to sleep with his wife while his men were out fighting and dying in battle. So to cover his sin, David conspired with another commander in the army to commit murder. Uriah would be sent to the front lines just at the right time when the army would retreat. David knew that Uriah would be killed.

Have you ever tried to cover your tracks? Did the truth come out anyway? Explain.

How could all this have been avoided in David's life?

After Nathan the prophet confronted David with his sin, he pronounced a harsh reality and the consequences for David's sin. The only thing to do at this point was to confess and repent—agree with God about the condition of his heart and return to Him. And that's what David did.

[7] Nathan replied to David, "You are the man! This is what the LORD God of Israel says: 'I anointed you king over Israel, and I delivered you from the hand of Saul. [8] I gave your master's house to you and your master's wives into your arms, and I gave you the house of Israel and Judah, and if that was not enough, I would have given you even more. [9] Why then have you despised the command of the LORD by doing what I consider evil? You struck down Uriah the Hittite with the sword and took his wife as your own wife— you murdered him with the Ammonite's sword. [10] Now therefore, the sword will never leave your house because you despised Me and took the wife of Uriah the Hittite to be your own wife.'" [13] David responded to Nathan, "I have sinned against the LORD." Then Nathan replied to David, "The LORD has taken away your sin; you will not die. [14] However, because you treated the LORD with such contempt in this matter, the son born to you will die."

2 SAMUEL 12:7-10,13-14

In books and movies it doesn't matter how many mistakes the characters make because everything always works out in the end. But in real life when we do something stupid, it normally costs us. What consequences have you suffered as a result of poor choices you've made?

Did you anticipate the consequences before you chose the action? What would you do differently now?

God, help me to see the true reality of my situation. Give me a glimpse of my future, the consequences of my actions. Show me how to turn around and give me the faith to return to You. Amen.

AS YOU WISH

If you were granted one wish, what is the one thing you would want more than anything else?

When Solomon became king, the temple of God was not yet built. So the people were making sacrifices in "high places." These high places were raised areas that were dedicated to other gods. They were modeled after the Canaanite religions. The Bible says that Solomon walked in all of David's ways except that Solomon sacrificed in high places.

In spite of this, God appeared to Solomon and said, "Ask. What should I give you?" (2 Chronicles 1:7). Since Solomon asked for wisdom, he was given a wise and discerning heart as well as wealth and honor by God. As an added bonus, God gave Solomon another promise.

> If you walk in My ways and keep My statutes and commands
> just as your father David did, I will give you a long life.
> 1 KINGS 3:14

During Solomon's reign, wealth poured into Israel. After the completion of the temple, Solomon sacrificed thousands of animals, and there was a 14-day festival that all the people attended. Afterward, God appeared to Solomon again. He gave him the same promise. But this time, God issued a warning as well.

> 4 As for you, if you walk before Me as your father David
> walked, with a heart of integrity and in what is right, doing
> everything I have commanded you, and if you keep My
> statutes and ordinances, 5 I will establish your royal throne
> over Israel forever, as I promised your father David: You
> will never fail to have a man on the throne of Israel.
> 6 If you or your sons turn away from following Me and do not
> keep My commands—My statutes that I have set before you—
> and if you go and serve other gods and worship them, 7 I will cut
> off Israel from the land I gave them, and I will reject the temple
> I have sanctified for My name. Israel will become an object of

scorn and ridicule among all the peoples. [8] Though this temple
is now exalted, everyone who passes by will be appalled and
will mock. They will say: Why did the LORD do this to this land
and this temple? [9] Then they will say: Because they abandoned
the LORD their God who brought their ancestors out of the land
of Egypt. They clung to other gods and worshiped and served
them. Because of this, the LORD brought all this ruin on them.

1 KINGS 9:4-9

Solomon, for all of his wisdom, could not follow this command of the Lord. His
foreign wives turned his heart away from God, and he learned the ways of their
gods. Because of this, God came to him again and told him that because he did not
remember to walk in the way of David, the kingdom would be stripped from him and
Israel would be torn apart.

Over time, other nations rose against Israel and attacked. The peace they had known
under Solomon had come to an end. His son, Rehoboam, inherited the kingdom, and
he was inclined to be even harder on the people than Solomon. God's words rang
true once again. The kingdom fell apart.

> Have you ever seen the consequences of your actions before you committed
> them but chose to commit them anyway? Why?

Choose to think about the consequences of your actions before you disobey God.

---

*God, when I am tempted, remind me that I have the opportunity to obey before
I disobey. I want to follow You more and more each day. Amen.*

WHAT'S THE MEANING OF ALL OF THIS?

What brings life meaning for you?

Why do you think is it important for our lives and our endeavors to have meaning?

We've all heard stories of people having midlife crises. The sports car. The second marriage. The hairpiece. There is something about midlife that makes people start questioning everything about themselves and their legacy.

What have I done that is important? How will I be remembered? Do I regret not taking that risk?

Those who experience a midlife crisis see their lives as being half over, and more than likely they feel as though they don't have a lot to show for it.

Solomon had these same questions and issues. Though his kingdom was the richest and mightiest on earth, he considered everything he had done to be futile. He thought none of it would stand the test of time. Even the gift of wisdom that God had given him was a source of contention within him.

These are among the first words of Ecclesiastes. There's a heavy burden and weight upon Solomon. Even with all his knowledge and riches, even with all his wisdom, there's something missing in Solomon's life.

> [13] I applied my mind to seek and explore through wisdom
> all that is done under heaven. God has given people this
> miserable task to keep them occupied. [14] I have seen
> all the things that are done under the sun and have
> found everything to be futile, a pursuit of the wind.
> ECCLESIASTES 1:13-14

What could have been missing? Solomon had everything he ever wanted, and He pursued everything there was to pursue. He entertained himself with comedy and laughter. He got his hands dirty and went into construction building parks, highways, and mansions. He built a massive portfolio. He surrounded himself with the best entertainers of the day.

> [10] All that my eyes desired, I did not deny them. I did not refuse myself any pleasure, for I took pleasure in all my struggles. This was my reward for all my struggles. [11] When I considered all that I had accomplished and what I had labored to achieve, I found everything to be futile and a pursuit of the wind. There was nothing to be gained under the sun.
>
> ECCLESIASTES 2:10-11

When have you missed the blessings in front of you by continually pursuing more, only to end up with less?

What do you think you were searching for? What did you discover in that pursuit?

Regardless of his life, the one thing that Solomon could not escape was the certainty of death. At some point, no matter how rich or poor, wise or foolish, we all have an appointment with death. This is the sobering thought that will stop any rich, successful man in his tracks. Solomon had riches and wisdom to spare, but he could not overcome death and judgment.

God, help me to number my days and be a good steward of the time You have given me on earth. Help me avoid the futility of working hard toward temporary things. Show me what I need to do that will have eternal significance.

THE PREDICTIONS: KEEP GOD FIRST
2 KINGS–MALACHI

2 KINGS–MALACHI

Can you imagine what God's daytime planner would look like if He had one? Each page would be meticulously written with details concerning what to accomplish when and where. Prayers that need to be answered later are carried over to the next page. Never too busy or in a hurry, God would always be on time for every appointment. The illustration may be silly, but it does put things into perspective. We all have goals, strategies, appointments, interactions, and priorities.

Priorities. Have you ever thought about the priorities of God? At the end of the day, what does He want to accomplish in you for Himself? Nothing is going to get in His way. Job understood this when he said to God, "I know that You can do anything and no plan of Yours can be thwarted" (Job 42:2). But what are we doing about it? How are we aggressively cooperating with God to accomplish His purposes on this earth?

Elisabeth Elliot once said, "The will of God is not something you add to your life. It's a course you choose. You either line yourself up with the Son of God … or you capitulate to the principle which governs the rest of the world." She is right. When our schedules are full to the max with our priorities, how can we add God's will to our lives? It's impossible. We need to follow the commands of Jesus Christ. Since God wants to be number one in our lives, Jesus said to seek God's kingdom first. To seek the kingdom is to seek the King.

BACK TRACK

In your personal time this past week you read about David running from King Saul and how that taught him to run to God. What's happening in your life that's teaching you to run to God? Share your experience with your group.

FRAMING THE STORY

Which sport do you think is most difficult to remain on top? Why?

Boxing/MMA
Gymnastics
Soccer
Curling
Marathon running
Other: _____

Each sport has its own training regimen and competition, so there are different reasons why it's tough to stay on top and remain number one for each. Similarly, there are different things that make it difficult for us to keep God number one. Keep this in mind as you continue your small-group time.

2 Kings–Malachi

KEY POINTS

1. After Solomon's death, his kingdom was divided into two halves—the Northern Kingdom and the Southern Kingdom. They would remain divided for many years.
2. Jonah ran from God. He didn't want the Ninevites to repent.
3. The Southern Kingdom was a roller coaster ride of good kings and bad kings. A good king would move people toward God, and then several bad kings would drive the nation back down.
4. Daniel rose to influence in Babylon. He accurately predicted the next 600 years of history, including the rise of Persia, Alexander the Great, and the Roman Empire.
5. Daniel was thrown into the lion's den for seeking God. God delivered him supernaturally.
6. God had waited for the Babylonians to seek Him. The time for waiting was over; the time of consequences had come.
7. Esther became queen for "such a time as this."
8. Nehemiah felt prompted to leave his post and help the people return to God. He put together a strategic plan, got funding, and rebuilt the walls in record time.
9. The most significant predictions made by the prophets described the coming Messiah. These predictions were all made more than 400 years before Jesus stepped onto the scene of history.

NOTES

The following list is intriguing because these characters were pressed and pushed in every way, yet God used them to complete His purposes:

The kings were constantly on a spiritual roller coaster of ups and downs.

Daniel pursued God during some life-threatening situations.

Elijah struggled with depression.

Esther needed to display courage and bravery for a long period of time.

Jonah openly ran from God.

Nehemiah received God's wisdom to implement his personal calling/vision.

> Which experience do you think would be most difficult for you to endure? Explain.

> If God can use each of these people, what does this say about His desire to use you?

Even though some of our experiences in life seem unique to us, the feelings we encounter when we are tempted are common. The Bible says, "No temptation has overtaken you except what is common to humanity. God is faithful, and He will not allow you to be tempted beyond what you are able, but with the temptation He will also provide a way of escape so that you are able to bear it" (1 Corinthians 10:13).

Consider Jonah's story. We probably will not experience the trauma he did, but that doesn't mean we can't relate to Jonah's real problems in life—the ones that kept him from putting God first.

¹ Jonah was greatly displeased and became furious. ² He prayed to the LORD: "Please, LORD, isn't this what I said while I was still in my own country? That's why I fled toward Tarshish in the first place. I knew that You are a merciful and compassionate God, slow to become angry, rich in faithful love, and One who relents from sending disaster. ³ And now, LORD, please take my life from me, for it is better for me to die than to live."

JONAH 4:1-3

Look at the attributes of God that Jonah lists in verse 2. Why do you think Jonah would run from a God with these attributes?

Look again at the attributes of God listed in Jonah 4:2. Divide into groups of 2-3 and compile your own list. Come back together and share your lists in the larger group. Discuss the tension of putting and keeping God first.

You would think most preachers would be thrilled at the sight of an entire city repenting of their sin and choosing to follow God. Not Jonah. He knew the Ninevites would repent if he preached, but he was filled with such a hatred for them that he didn't want them to experience God's grace. The Ninevites were an Assyrian city, a longstanding enemy of the nation of Israel. Known for their cruelty, when the Ninevites would capture a city they would behead the men and sacrifice the women and children.

Have you ever been upset about something God asked you to do? Why?

The landscape of life requires that our journey with God remain adaptable. We initiate and respond to certain situations, people, places, and experiences. Sharing our lives with people we love can help shape our God-first attitude. Sharing our lives with people who stir up conflict and strife can also help our ability to keep God number one.

> [8] Then Haman informed King Ahasuerus, "There is one ethnic group, scattered throughout the peoples in every province of your kingdom, yet living in isolation. Their laws are different from everyone else's and they do not obey the king's laws. It is not in the king's best interest to tolerate them. [9] If the king approves, let an order be drawn up authorizing their destruction, and I will pay 375 tons of silver to the accountants for deposit in the royal treasury."
>
> ESTHER 3:8-9

> [4:14] If you keep silent at this time, liberation and deliverance will come to the Jewish people from another place, but you and your father's house will be destroyed. Who knows, perhaps you have come to your royal position for such a time as this.
>
> ESTHER 4:14

Look at how Esther managed very real conflict. What is the cost of putting God first? What does keeping God first require of them?

What distractions did Esther most likely have to deal with in this scenario?

List the distractions in your life that make it difficult for you to keep God first.

WRAP

Distractions come in many shapes and sizes. They can present themselves as beautiful and enticing, ordinary and mundane, or ugly and hateful. We can be drawn away from God by indulging in sinful activity. We can be drawn away from God by averting righteous actions. We can veer off course even when we obey God if we do the right thing for the wrong reason. Keeping God first isn't just a matter of willpower; it is a matter of the mind and heart. And we've seen this played out both positively and negatively in 2 Kings—Malachi.

There were distractions. There was punishment. There were kings who longed to draw their people to God and others who worked to push Him away. But all of these stories point to one thing: God was always working—in advance—to protect and provide for His people.

Have you ever wondered if the Bible is reliable? If it's true? If so, I hope some of your doubt has diminished during your study this week. Chad spent a significant amount of time in his video message pointing out all the predictions made and fulfilled.

Pick one question, contradiction, or idea that is of particular interest to you and spend some time in your Bible this week investigating it. Your confidence in God will go up when your confidence in His Word goes up.

The Bible is reliable. The Bible is true. And God wants us to know His truth because it is only that truth that can set us free.

God, help us to see people the way You see them. Teach us what it means to put You first in all we do, even how we treat those who are against us. We want to put You first even when we don't know how. We surrender all of our relationships to You. Help us navigate them so that You remain first in everything. Amen.

PERSONAL TRACK

GETTING OUR ATTENTION

In the past, how has God gotten your attention? Think of a time when you were really aware that God was interested in your life and write about it here.

After Solomon died and the kingdom was divided, evil kings rose up and constantly led the people to worship false gods. To battle the false gods, the One True God raised up prophets who preached the truth and performed wondrous signs. Elijah was the first of these prophets. This was the spiritually corrupt culture in which Elijah bursts onto the scene and begins his public ministry. His bombastic approach and sharp words are worthy of notice.

One time Elijah declared a drought to punish the nation for its idolatry (1 Kings 17-18). The drought ended in a contest between Elijah and the Baal prophets. Elijah called fire down from heaven, and the prophets of Baal were defeated. Another time, Elijah came to King Ahab with a terrible prophecy of doom (1 Kings 21). The king had a man killed so he could steal his vineyard. Listen to this judgment:

> ¹⁷ Then the word of the LORD came to Elijah the Tishbite:
> ¹⁸ "Get up and go to meet Ahab king of Israel, who is in Samaria.
> You'll find him in Naboth's vineyard, where he has gone to
> take possession of it. ¹⁹ Tell him, 'This is what the LORD says:
> Have you murdered and also taken possession?' Then tell
> him, 'This is what the LORD says: In the place where the dogs
> licked Naboth's blood, the dogs will also lick your blood!'"
> ²⁰ Ahab said to Elijah, "So, you have caught me, my enemy."
> He replied, "I have caught you because you devoted
> yourself to do what is evil in the Lord's sight. ²¹ This
> is what the Lord says: 'I am about to bring disaster
> on you and will sweep away your descendants:

I will eliminate all of Ahab's males,
both slave and free, in Israel;

²² I will make your house like the house of Jeroboam son
of Nebat and like the house of Baasha son of Ahijah,
because you have provoked My anger and caused
Israel to sin. ²³ The Lord also speaks of Jezebel: The
dogs will eat Jezebel in the plot of land at Jezreel:

²⁴ He who belongs to Ahab and dies in the city, the dogs will eat,
and he who dies in the field, the birds of the sky will eat.'"

1 KINGS 21:17-24

Why do you think God's judgment is so harsh? How would you respond to a judgment like this?

What distracts you most from keeping God first?

King Ahab actually repented of his sin, and God had mercy on him. Because of Ahab's humility, God temporarily delayed His judgment and let Ahab live.

God, give me ears to hear You even when You whisper. I want to keep You first always. Help me keep my focus on You.

NAME THAT TUNE

Do you ever catch yourself singing a song that's in your head? How did it get there?

It's hard to keep God first when things around us are falling apart. We experience broken relationships with our families or friends. Our financial position isn't as strong as we would like for it to be. We look back at some of the decisions we have made and wish they weren't so. The busted world around us can slowly creep in and steal our joy. And when that happens, we focus on the wrong things and God takes second place.

The Book of Habakkuk was written during a time of international crisis for the nation of Israel. Babylonia was an emerging world power, and they would soon overtake God's people. There was corruption within the leadership of the nation. The kings were evil, ungodly, and rebellious, and social decay had given way to violence, greed, and perverted justice. So, it is no surprise that Habakkuk begins his book with a complaint.

Complaining is a difficult art to master. If we complain too much to God, we don't position ourselves to listen. If we vent to others, it may turn into gossip or a woe-is-me pity party. But here is the beauty we glean from Habakkuk's story: God listens and cares about our complaints and frustrations. God knows our hearts and He wants to engage us even when our hearts are low.

If you read this three-chapter book, you see that Habakkuk was truly burdened about his circumstances, and he was frustrated at the success of his enemies. He was confused about God's timing, judgment, and plan. After he complained twice to God, the Lord responded to him. Habakkuk listened to God—not just with his ears, but also with his heart. Then he stopped complaining and began to sing his song.

> [2] Lord, I stand in awe of Your deeds.
> Revive Your work in these years;
> make it known in these years.
> In Your wrath remember mercy!
> [17] Though the fig tree does not bud
> and there is no fruit on the vines,
> though the olive crop fails
> and the fields produce no food,

though there are no sheep in the pen
and no cattle in the stalls,
[18] yet I will triumph in Yahweh;
I will rejoice in the God of my salvation!
[19] Yahweh my LORD is my strength;
He makes my feet like those of a deer
and enables me to walk on mountain heights!
HABAKKUK 3:2,17-19

This is the song that was on Habakkuk's heart. Habakkuk saw two realities. The first centered on the circumstances around him. The second centered on the God who sees and knows all. It took complaining to God about the first reality to land on the second.

It's OK to complain to God as long as you want to truly dialogue with Him. God is not interested in monologues or one-way rants.

Thinking about God all day is like having your favorite rock anthem playing over and over in your head.

[18] Be filled by the Spirit:
[19] speaking to one another
in psalms, hymns, and spiritual songs,
singing and making music
from your heart to the Lord,
[20] giving thanks always for everything
to God the Father
in the name of our Lord Jesus Christ.
EPHESIANS 5:18-20

God, help me keep a song in my heart for You. No matter how bad it gets, don't let me lose my joy, my song, and trust in You. Amen.

DANIEL

The time of Daniel was not a bright point in the history of Judah. They had been ruled by Assyria for many years, but the Babylonians had risen in power and defeated Assyria. The Babylonians marched into Jerusalem, destroying the city walls and the temple, and deported the majority of the most important citizens. The aim was to educate the exiles in the Babylonian ways so that they would not rise up and rebel against King Nebuchadnezzar. Daniel was one of these exiles.

As part of his re-education, Daniel was asked to learn a new language and customs, change his name from Daniel to Belteshazzar, change his diet, and worship false idols. As a godly man, Daniel refused, and even though he was to be an advisor in the king's court, the king promised him and his friends, Hananiah, Mishael, and Azariah (Shadrach, Meshach, and Abednego) a terrible death if they would not comply with the Babylonian customs.

> Have you ever been ostracized or mistreated because of a stand you took for God? How hard was it to keep God first during this time?

Because Daniel and his friends would not defile themselves with the king's food and drink, God blessed them greatly. Daniel earned favor with the king and became a trusted confidant. The king sought him out concerning troubling dreams, and Daniel was very forthcoming with his interpretation of the dreams. Daniel gave God all the glory for showing him the dreams of the king and what they meant, and the king gave glory to God as well upon hearing Daniel's interpretation. He placed Daniel and his friends in high places within the kingdom as a reward for easing his troubled heart.

But this didn't stop Nebuchadnezzar from making a golden idol and commanding everyone to worship it. When the music played, everyone was to bow before the idol and worship it. Daniel's friends refused. The king was outraged:

> [16] Shadrach, Meshach, and Abednego replied to the king, "Nebuchadnezzar, we don't need to give you an answer to this question. [17] If the God we serve exists, then He can rescue us from the furnace of blazing fire, and He can rescue

us from the power of you, the king. ¹⁸ But even if He does
not rescue us, we want you as king to know that we will not
serve your gods or worship the gold statue you set up."
¹⁹ Then Nebuchadnezzar was filled with rage, and the
expression on his face changed toward Shadrach,
Meshach, and Abednego. He gave orders to heat the
furnace seven times more than was customary,
²⁰ and he commanded some of the strongest soldiers in his
army to tie up Shadrach, Meshach, and Abednego and throw
them into the furnace of blazing fire. ²¹ So these men, in their
trousers, robes, head coverings, and other clothes, were tied up
and thrown into the furnace of blazing fire. ²² Since the king's
command was so urgent and the furnace extremely hot, the
raging flames killed those men who carried Shadrach, Meshach,
and Abednego up. ²³ And these three men, Shadrach, Meshach,
and Abednego fell, bound, into the furnace of blazing fire.

DANIEL 3:16-23

As he waited for the screams, King Nebuchadnezzar looked and noticed that instead
of three people in the furnace, there were four—the three he had thrown in and one
who looked like "a son of the gods" (Daniel 3:25). When he removed the men from
the fire, he praised God and decreed that no one should speak a word against Him.
Because Daniel and his three friends took a stand for God by refusing to go against
His Word they were protected and rewarded. Further, Daniel was trusted and loved
by kings and rulers.

Who have you influenced for God? How can you encourage others to follow
Him through difficult times?

Think of a time when God blessed you because of your faithfulness to Him.
Take a moment to thank God for His goodness.

*Thank You, God, for being with me through the struggles and strife. I can't live this
life without You. Amen.*

GOD CAN USE ANYBODY

We read about a shepherd boy slaying a giant and becoming king.

We read about a widowed daughter-in-law finding provision with God's people.

We read about three men surviving an execution in the fiery furnace.

Today we will read about a young girl whose beauty captures the heart of the King of Persia.

In a nearby land, there lived a young orphan girl named Esther. She was sweet and beautiful, and she loved the Lord. Her cousin, Mordecai, who took her in and treated her as his own child, had raised her. When he received word of the king's search for a new queen, he knew his cousin would be taken to King Xerxes, since she was one of such rare beauty. Mordecai instructed her to do all that was asked of her and all would go well. He warned her, however, to remain quiet about her ancestry, as he did not want that to be the one thing that kept her from the king's favor. When King Xerxes met Esther, he loved her more than anyone else who had been brought before him, and he chose her for his new queen.

> [17] The king loved Esther more than all the other women. She won more favor and approval from him than did any of the other young women. He placed the royal crown on her head and made her queen in place of Vashti. [18] The king held a great banquet for all his officials and staff. It was Esther's banquet. He freed his provinces from tax payments and gave gifts worthy of the king's bounty.
> ESTHER 2:17-18

From David to Daniel's three friends, it seems that God prefers to use the young and humble to do His work and confound the strong and proud. Now He's picking a young girl to be queen.

How have you seen God use the "least of these" to accomplish His purposes in this world?

Meanwhile, the king put a new nobleman, Haman, into a high position in his kingdom. Haman was evil, and he decreed that all should bow down to him. But Mordecai refused. He bowed to no man. As was the custom of his people, he would bow only to God. Because of this, Haman declared that Mordecai would die, along with all of his people. King Xerxes agreed and set the date for the punishment. He unknowingly sentenced his own queen to death.

To save her cousin and her people, Esther needed to approach the king, reveal the plot, and request that their lives be spared. The problem is, no one is allowed to approach the king unless they are summoned. Not even the queen. But Esther risked her life not once but twice by going before the king. She was intent on saving her people. And God's chosen people were granted a stay of execution because of her.

What if God asked you to do something courageous like stand up to a powerful political figure? How would you respond?

Is there a young person in your life you can encourage? What would be your advice as he or she follows God?

Spend some time this week reading the rest of the story. The Book of Esther is only 10 chapters long and has a great ending.

God, help me to have the faith to do the things I profess to believe, standing strong through the good times and the bad. Amen.

MINOR PROPHETS

"How many times do I have to tell you?"

Did your parents ever ask you this? What are your memories of why?

The minor prophets are a collection of 12 books in the Old Testament. They are "minor" only in size, not in message. In their own unique way, the minor prophets echoed the message from God to the nation of Israel. Throughout their history, God was constantly calling the Israelites to keep Him first. It's God's way of telling His children, "How many times do I have to tell you? Keep Me first!"

Hosea revealed that God loves backsliders and He wants us to return to Him.

Joel warned that the day of Yahweh is coming, and we need to repent.

Amos' message focused on this: Be ready to meet God. He is the just Judge!

Obadiah preached that God's kingdom is forever. We need to live in it.

Jonah's actions taught that God loves everybody, even our enemies. Our hearts need to be right with God.

Micah brought hope to God's people. Expect God to do great things!

Nahum was confident that God would overthrow and defeat our enemies.

Habakkuk encouraged the people to walk by faith. Evil will be conquered.

Zephaniah promised there would be a remnant for God. Some will return.

Haggai said to find strength and stay courageous in discouraging times.

Zechariah reminded us that it's not always going to be like this. God's future is full of glory.

Malachi told us when we rob God, we offend Him. He wants us to trust Him with everything.

How have these messages applied to your own life? Which message resonates with your heart the most right now? Explain.

Let whoever is wise understand these things,
and whoever is insightful recognize them.
For the ways of the LORD are right,
and the righteous walk in them,
but the rebellious stumble in them.
HOSEA 14:9

Mankind, He has told you what is good
and what it is the LORD requires of you:
to act justly,
to love faithfulness,
and to walk humbly with your God.
MICAH 6:8

Look, his ego is inflated;
he is without integrity.
But the righteous one will live by his faith.
HABAKKUK 2:4

Walking with God takes wisdom, humility, and faith. Which of these passages do you need to pursue most? How will you do that?

God, help me develop a lifestyle of wisdom and faith. Show me how to be humble as I live for You and serve others in Your name. Amen.

Fast Track

Session 5

THE DOUBTS: FACING ADVERSITY

JOB, RUTH, LAMENTATIONS, PSALMS

JOB, RUTH, LAMENTATIONS, PSALMS

> "Doubts and mistrust are the mere panic of timid imagination, which the steadfast heart will conquer, and the large mind transcend."
> HELEN KELLER

The question isn't, *Are we going to be confronted with doubt?* The question is, *What are we going to do about doubt?* We all have bouts with doubt. It's easy to start doubting God when we experience suffering. It's easy to lose sight of the fact that God is good when the relationships around us go bad. It's easy to get worn out with worry when our world begins to unravel.

What's difficult is maintaining a consistent faith in God that refuses to allow doubt to creep in and wreak havoc. If the worry-free life was easy, everybody would be doing it. But New Testament and Old Testament saints alike wrestled with their own challenges and personal doubts. Their faith in God was stretched, challenged, and put to the test. Some of them experienced short-term frustration. Others felt the unrelenting cloak of long-term weariness.

As you move through this session, look for those believers who continued to engage God in the midst of their adversity and let God show you how you can do the same. Let the Holy Spirit replace fear with faith. Let the Scripture do its work—a total transformation of the timid imagination.

Be encouraged. We who doubt are not alone.

BACK TRACK

Last week's session was all about keeping God first. What has God been teaching you through your personal study this past week? Briefly discuss any of the following:

How has God gotten your attention?
Has God asked you to do something difficult for Him?
What are you learning about loving your enemies?
How do you see God working and accomplishing His purposes in your life?

FRAMING THE STORY

Think about your favorite movie characters and how they may have expressed doubt. Some examples are listed below. Some of these movies are based on true stories. How do they compare with each other? How do they portray real life?

Lieutenant Dan (played by Gary Sinise in *Forrest Gump*)
Evan Baxter (played by Steve Carell in *Evan Almighty*)
William Wilberforce (played by Ioan Gruffudd in *Amazing Grace*)
Dr. Eleanor "Ellie" Arroway (played by Jodie Foster in *Contact*)
Grant Taylor (played by Alex Kendrick in *Facing the Giants*)
Other: _____

VIDEO TRACK

Job, Ruth, Lamentations, Psalms

KEY POINTS

1. In the midst of Job's pain, he worshiped. "Blessed be the name of the Lord. He gives and takes away."
2. Job's four friends came to "comfort" him in his pain.
3. God came down to Job to give him what he asked for—an audience with his Creator. While God never answered Job's questions directly, God revealed that He can be trusted during tragedy. God reminded Job that He loved him dearly.
4. Naomi's faith tank was empty, her emotions exhausted. She was bitter at God. Naomi had given up on God; however, God had not given up on Naomi.
5. Habakkuk had a choice: he could cling to God, trusting Him to know best, or curse God for allowing the pain to continue. Habakkuk was given freedom to struggle, doubt, and cry in the struggle.
6. Jeremiah felt like God had targeted his people. He felt like he had no hope, no comfort, no future, and no God on his side. But God was faithful.
7. The Book of Psalms reminds us to cry out to God in times of need.
8. We serve a God who walks with us during the dark times, like a good shepherd who leads us to greener pastures.
9. The God of the Bible doesn't stay up in heaven looking down from a distance. God will come close. He will enter into our pain.

NOTES

GROUP TRACK

Think about the biblical stories and characters that Chad spoke of in his video message this week. They all had different ways of responding to pain and suffering:

Job's friends: "When we experience bad things, it's like karma. What goes around comes around."

Naomi: "My bad experience and personal pain have left my emotional tank empty."

Habakkuk: "I don't understand how good people can suffer while wicked people are never persecuted."

Lamentations: "I know there's pain in the world, and I empathize with people who are struggling right now."

What do these perspectives have in common? How do they differ?

Look at the following questions. Once the crisis hits, which question do you ask God first?

God, why is this happening to me?
God, what are You trying to teach me?
God, who are You trying to reach because of this?
God, where are You in all of this?
God, when is this going to end?

As we experience the ups and downs of life in this broken world, doubt and disbelief can creep into our hearts. When the crisis moments hit our lives, we can either cling to God or curse God. How we respond to Him (and the questions we ask Him) will determine which course we take.

¹ During the time of the judges, there was a famine in the land.
A man left Bethlehem in Judah with his wife and two sons
to live in the land of Moab for a while. ² The man's name was
Elimelech, and his wife's name was Naomi. They entered the
land of Moab and settled there. ³ Naomi's husband Elimelech
died, and she was left with her two sons. ⁴ Her sons took
Moabite women as their wives: one was named Orpah and
the second was named Ruth. After they lived in Moab about
10 years, ⁵ both Mahlon and Chilion also died, and Naomi was
left without her two children and without her husband.

RUTH 1:1-5

Describe the adversity that Naomi was facing in these opening verses of Ruth.
What is today's equivalent?

Consider what Chad shared in his message this week regarding Naomi's story.
What can you learn from how she handled her situation—both what to do and
what not to do?

¹⁸ When Naomi saw that Ruth was determined to go
with her, she stopped trying to persuade her.
¹⁹ The two of them traveled until they came to Bethlehem. When
they entered Bethlehem, the whole town was excited about their
arrival and the local women exclaimed, "Can this be Naomi?"
²⁰ "Don't call me Naomi. Call me Mara," she answered,
"for the Almighty has made me very bitter. ²¹ I went
away full, but the Lord has brought me back empty. Why
do you call me Naomi, since the Lord has pronounced
judgment on me, and the Almighty has afflicted me?"

RUTH 1:18-21

Do you remember a time when you were at the end of your rope like Naomi?
How did you respond?

Like Naomi, Job and the apostle Paul also suffered many hardships while living for
God. Both men found a way through their tough times to find God. In his own personal journey, Paul got to the point where he could express a certain desire of his
heart. At the end of Job's story, he also made an incredible summary statement, so
to speak, about what he had experienced.

> My goal is to know Him and the power of His resurrection and
> the fellowship of His sufferings, being conformed to His death.
> PHILIPPIANS 3:10

Why do you think we can know Jesus at a deeper level through suffering,
as Paul stated?

> [2] I know that You can do anything
> and no plan of Yours can be thwarted ...
> [3] Surely I spoke about things I did not understand,
> things too wonderful for me to know.
> [5] I had heard rumors about You,
> but now my eyes have seen You.
> JOB 42:2-3,5

Both Paul and Job recognized that knowing Jesus on a deeper level is brought
about through suffering. Discuss how this frame of mind can put you on the
right track to keep the doubt away.

How have you come to know God in your own life? In what ways does your
"knowing" influence the way you handle doubt and adversity?

WRAP

What do you do when you're going through a difficult time? When you face adversity do you curse God or cling to Him? What thoughts take you captive?

> Let us run with endurance the race that lies before us, keeping
> our eyes on Jesus, the source and perfecter of our faith.
> HEBREWS 12:1-2

Especially when we're in the midst of the battle, we can confidently fix our eyes on the One who was there in the beginning and will be there to the end. Our God is good. He is trustworthy. And He is with us ... always.

George MacDonald (19th century Scottish author/poet) wrote, "To be trusted is a greater compliment than being loved." Trusting God is an act of loving God that leads us to knowing God. We may not understand the full weight and wisdom of a God who sees a broken world suffering from sin, but we can choose to understand that these hardships can be the means to the best end.

Spend time going deeper into some of the stories we've looked at this week. Use their doubts and questions to give you the confidence to be honest with God about yours.

God, we know You are big enough to handle all of our questions. If doubt begins to creep in, show us where You are in our lives. Remind us of the good questions to ask. Help us to be patient with You as You answer them in Your own timing. Amen.

PERSONAL TRACK

JOB'S FRIENDS

> There is a friend who stays closer than a brother.
> PROVERBS 18:24

Think about a time when a close friend judged you. How did that affect you? How did it affect your relationship?

Job was a very blessed man. The Bible portrays him as one of perfect integrity, a man who turned away from evil. He was the greatest man among all the people of the east. He was wealthy and well regarded and had many sons and daughters whom he loved very much. Job's story, though, begins with a conversation between God and Satan.

> [8] Then the LORD said to Satan, "Have you considered My servant Job? No one else on earth is like him, a man of perfect integrity, who fears God and turns away from evil." [9] Satan answered the LORD, "Does Job fear God for nothing? [10] Haven't You placed a hedge around him, his household, and everything he owns? You have blessed the work of his hands, and his possessions have increased in the land. [11] But stretch out Your hand and strike everything he owns, and he will surely curse You to Your face." [12] "Very well," the LORD told Satan, "everything he owns is in your power. However, you must not lay a hand on Job himself." So Satan left the LORD's presence.
> JOB 1:8-12

God gave Satan control over everything in Job's life, and in the blink of an eye it was all gone—his wealth, his children, even his own health. And Job's reaction was to praise God. In fact, throughout all his trials Job didn't sin or blame God for anything.

After awhile, Job's friends began to appear. Eliphaz, Bildad, and Zophar sat with him for seven days, not saying a single word. When the seven days were over, they began to speak, and the incriminations began to roll. Each of the three men believed beyond a doubt that Job was not quite as righteous as he was pretending to be or as everyone thought he was.

Eliphaz thought Job was suffering because he hadn't done enough good. He believed that God was too far above the people to see and care, and that evil always resulted in punishment.

Bildad believed that since Job was suffering, he had been unrighteous, because God punishes wicked people. He believed that Job's children died because they were sinful.

Zophar's attitude was almost one of anger toward Job. He believed Job was suffering because he had done evil. He felt that if Job wanted things to be the way they had been, Job would have to repent and God would restore him.

> Have you ever been in a position where you jumped to judgment about something or someone? Explain.

Job denied any wrongdoing over and over, but his friends would not listen. In their eyes suffering only came to the wicked, and Job was suffering. He must be hiding something. But Job knew he had not done wrong, that he was blameless.

The final friend, Elihu, disagreed. Elihu told the three others that they were wrong. They didn't understand the true nature of God—that He was holy and blameless. Job was not blameless, but God is. Both the righteous and the wicked prosper and suffer. And God is above them all.

Job's friends were miserable comforters. Regardless of their motives, they only added to Job's trial. Yet Job "prayed for his friends" (42:10). And it was at this point that God restored Job—and gave him twice what he had before.

> Job came to know God deeply, not simply to know about Him. How will you allow your struggles to change your relationships?

God, help me to listen to You and to my friends who are wise and will tell me the truth. Help me to filter out those who would just make me doubt You. Amen.

JOB'S UPS AND DOWNS

[20] Then Job stood up, tore his robe, and shaved his
head. He fell to the ground and worshiped, [21] saying:

Naked I came from my mother's womb,
and naked I will leave this life.
The Lord gives, and the Lord takes away.
Praise the name of Yahweh.
[22] Throughout all this Job did not sin
or blame God for anything.
JOB 1:20-22

When it comes to experiencing suffering and adversity, people who know the Bible generally think of the story of Job. There isn't another book in the Bible where a person is so candid with God, where a person shares his deepest grief with God and pours out his heart. But there are aspects of the story that we sometimes miss.

Chapter 1 says that Job was a righteous and blameless man. He was protected and blessed by God. And when Satan destroyed his wealth and took away his children, it says that Job fell on the ground and worshiped God. And in that he did not sin.

But Job was not a perfect man and as we read his lament, we find there is a change in his heart. After Job lost everything, Satan attacked his person. He put painful boils on his body and Job was shunned from society. Job was alone and suffering. Friends visited him but mostly brought judgment and condemnation.

Job defended his position to his friends. He was innocent and blameless. But as he began to get more and more honest with God, he turned from blameless to bitter.

I am disgusted with my life.
I will express my complaint
and speak in the bitterness of my soul.
JOB 10:1

Job not only became bitter, but he began to freely voice his complaints. This is why we must be very careful with our words. Job was a righteous and blameless man, but his problems revealed something in his heart.

Luke 6:45 says that the "mouth speaks from the overflow of the heart." Job began to complain, which gave way to sin in his heart. He focused more on his circumstances than on God and the more he complained, the more his worship turned to accusation. Job no longer worshiped God. In the quietness of his heart, he blamed God for his suffering.

God held nothing back from Job in His response. The Word says that God's response comes in a whirlwind. As God spoke, Job came face to face with the righteousness of Almighty God. God said in Job 40:2, "Will the one who contends with the Almighty correct Him?" At this point Job clearly saw his sin and came to God broken and repentant. And what the Enemy had taken away, God restored.

> Do you ever doubt the goodness of God? In what ways has your doubt turned to bitterness?

> Has there been a time you blamed God for your circumstances? Be honest with yourself and with God.

Holy Spirit, please reveal to me any place in my heart that has turned bitter. I want my relationship with You to be completely restored. Amen.

RUTH AND NAOMI

When was the last time you just knew God was going to come through for you—no doubt in your mind? How did you know?

The Book of Ruth tells a story of adversity and faithfulness. It is a story of human suffering and a God who stood beside His people. There had been a severe famine in Israel during the time of the Judges. The people were migrating out of the land in search of sustenance. Naomi, her husband, Elimelech, and their two sons ended up in Moab. Naomi's husband died there, and the sons both married Moabite women.

After about 10 years, both sons died, leaving all three women alone. Naomi decided to return to her homeland, possibly thinking a relative there could provide for her. She spoke to both her daughters-in-law, advising them to return to their homes as well. Eventually, Orpah did return to her home, but Ruth refused to leave Naomi's side. Ruth chose to leave her father and mother and her own country and go to a foreign land instead. She turned away from her gods and chose to worship the only God. There seemed to be no doubt in her mind.

When we think of Ruth, the word that comes to mind is *steadfast*—resolutely or dutifully firm and unwavering. Ruth's loyalty to Naomi was unwavering. Nothing looked more bleak than the situation in which Ruth found herself. Her husband was dead. Her mother-in-law was without her husband and sons. There was no one to provide for them. There was no one to care for them.

But Ruth didn't think twice about the hardships she and Naomi would face with no one to care for them. Not once in this story did Ruth ever complain or turn bitter. She never blamed God for the tragedy that had fallen on her family. In fact, she walked in uncommon grace.

In order to help take care of herself and Naomi, Ruth would gather the leftovers from a field owned by Boaz—a relative of Noami's husband. The Word says she was there at sunrise and worked until sunset. Boaz noticed her and knew about all the things she had done for her mother-in-law. And because of that, Ruth found favor in his eyes. Boaz allowed her to work in his field, and he provided protection and provision for her.

[8] Boaz said to Ruth, "Listen, my daughter. Don't go and gather grain in another field, and don't leave this one, but stay here close to my female servants. [9] See which field they are harvesting, and follow them. Haven't I ordered the young men not to touch you? When you are thirsty, go and drink from the jars the young men have filled." [10] She bowed with her face to the ground and said to him, "Why are you so kind to notice me, although I am a foreigner?" [11] Boaz answered her, "Everything you have done for your mother-in-law since your husband's death has been fully reported to me: how you left your father and mother and the land of your birth, and how you came to a people you didn't previously know. [12] May the LORD reward you for what you have done, and may you receive a full reward from the LORD God of Israel, under whose wings you have come for refuge."

RUTH 2:8-12

So Ruth worked from sunrise to sunset, trusting that God would provide for her and Naomi. She didn't let her circumstances discourage her to the point of doubting God.

Have you ever found yourself doubting God's provision? Why do you think Ruth never seemed to have those doubts?

God, thank You for reminding me of Your ultimate provision. Help me to trust You without a doubt. Amen.

LAMENT AND VENT

Where do you air your gripes most often—family, friends, social media, God?

Everyone needs a person or place to vent their sorrow and anger. Some people think Facebook is the place to lament and vent to the world. The next time you or your friends gripe about life on Facebook, remember this story. The sorrow found in this appropriately-titled book, Lamentations, is worth its weight in grief.

Most likely Jeremiah wrote the book. He was a prophet in Judah during the reign of King Josiah. Under Josiah, the nation had begun to do away with idol worship and return to God. Jeremiah and other prophets helped by preaching against the sins of the people and asking them to repent and return to God.

After the death of Josiah, the nation again returned to idol worship. This broke Jeremiah's heart, and he had to tell the people what the consequences of their sin would be—they would be invaded from the north, and everything would be destroyed. The people would be exiled from their homeland. The Book of Lamentations picks up the story after this destruction has occurred, while Judah is in exile.

At this point, the conditions in Jerusalem are horrible. Jeremiah was grieving over all the things he witnessed during this time. The city was in ruin. Death was all around. Starving people were eating their own children to survive. Jeremiah's calling was to restore the people to God, to bring hope. But it seemed there was no hope for anyone. God's judgment had fallen, and they were being destroyed.

What things are most likely to break your heart?

What most often drives you to God with sorrow?

In spite of everything, Jeremiah remained hopeful. Looking back, he had seen the terrible wrath of God. He had seen the destruction of his people. He had seen them removed from the land God had given them. But God had protected them from total destruction. A remnant of people remained, and Jeremiah remained hopeful.

> ²² Because of the LORD's faithful love
> we do not perish,
> for His mercies never end.
> ²³ They are new every morning;
> great is Your faithfulness!
> LAMENTATIONS 3:22-23

Once hope was restored, once the people returned to God, Jeremiah knew that God would bring justice to the ones who had brought such sorrow to His people. He prayed that God would defend them against their enemies and that He would pay them back in like kind for what they had done to His people.

Jeremiah's final petition was prayer for restoration. He had seen the devastation. He had heard the screaming, the crying. And now he was praying for it to end and for God to respond in mercy. The people of Judah were as widows and orphans, and Jeremiah prayed that God would meet their needs.

Are you ever hesitant to lament and vent to God? Explain.

What can we learn about God's character from the Book of Lamentations?

God, no matter how bad it gets, I am not going to doubt Your plan and purpose for my life or Your love for me. I love You. Amen.

PSALMS

¹ Be gracious to me, God, be gracious to me,
for I take refuge in You.
I will seek refuge in the shadow of Your wings
until danger passes.
² I call to God Most High,
to God who fulfills His purpose for me.
PSALM 57:1-2

It seemed like everything was turning out well for David. He was the youngest of Jesse's sons, a shepherd, anointed by God to be king. He killed Goliath and became famous. King Saul embraced him ... at first. But when the people began to favor David over Saul, jealousy filled Saul's heart and things began to go very wrong for David.

When the Spirit of God left Saul and stripped him from his anointing to be king, he became a madman on the hunt for David. The only thing David knew to do was flee. He fled to the cave of Adullam and Psalm 142 gives us a glimpse of how he felt.

¹ I cry aloud to the LORD;
I plead aloud to the LORD for mercy.
² I pour out my complaint before Him;
I reveal my trouble to Him.
³ Although my spirit is weak within me,
You know my way.
Along this path I travel
they have hidden a trap for me.
⁴ Look to the right and see:
no one stands up for me;
there is no refuge for me;
no one cares about me.
⁵ I cry to You, LORD;
I say, "You are my shelter,
my portion in the land of the living."
PSALM 142:1-5

When you find yourself in what feels like an impossible situation, do you most often try to fix it or cry out to God and allow Him to rescue you? What do you think motivates you to react the way you do?

God had made a promise to David that he would be king, but on the road to that destiny David found himself alone and afraid. He thought he would die in that cave. But as he began to cry out to the Lord, something happened: David's pleas turned to praise.

> [8] Wake up, my soul!
> Wake up, harp and lyre!
> I will wake up the dawn.
> [9] I will praise You, Lord, among the peoples;
> I will sing praises to You among the nations.
> PSALM 57:8-9

In that lonely, solitary cave, David found refuge in God and God alone. God brought David to a solitary place to give him hope and strength.

Where is the special solitary place you go when you need to hear from God? Why is that place important to you?

God wants to speak to you. He wants to give you that same hope and strength He gave David. If you listen, you will hear.

How do you approach God in those quiet, solitary moments? How do you position yourself to hear?

Let your prayer be like David's: *God, I want my prayers to turn to praise. I want the anguish in my heart to come out as a song to You. Amen.*

THE CHRIST: GOD'S GREATEST GIFT

MATTHEW–JOHN

MATTHEW–JOHN

"Knowing God without knowing our own wretchedness makes for pride. Knowing our own wretchedness without knowing God makes for despair. Knowing Jesus Christ strikes the balance because he shows us both God and our own wretchedness."
BLAISE PASCAL

How great is this gift of Jesus Christ? The perfect Man meets the most imperfect world. Jesus is the bold collision between the Divine One and the desperate ones. He is great enough to be the Savior of the world but personal enough to be our Lord and Savior.

Jesus brings the greatest opportunity for all mankind. When we read His words in the Gospels, we quickly understand that He is the only way to the Father. The Father's heart is to reach all people. And this gift is open to all.

This session is all about the gift of Jesus Christ. Jesus' life from the cradle to the cross and beyond is found in four small books in the New Testament. As we navigate through the Gospel accounts, pay attention to the relationship Jesus had with the Father and how Jesus obeyed Him. Watch how God unwraps this gift to the entire world. There was no pomp and circumstance, just humility and goodness, miracles and love.

Witness how those around Jesus responded to Him. The poor loved that He was so accessible. The hungry were fed and followed Him. His home-town rejected Him but society's outcasts accepted Him. His disciples learned from Him. Sinners welcomed His message of hope and forgiveness. The religious elites rejected Him and ultimately crucified Him on the cross.

But Jesus lives again. He lives today and forever. How will you respond to the gift today? What will you do with Jesus tomorrow?

BACK TRACK

Your personal devotions over the past week likely provoked some thoughts about doubting God. Have you found a healthy way to lament and vent when things go wrong? How has your faith in God's provision increased and your doubt decreased? Take a few minutes to share.

FRAMING THE STORY

What's a favorite gift you received for your birthday, Christmas, or other special occasion? What's a favorite gift you gave? Explain to your group what made these gifts so significant.

▶ VIDEO TRACK

Matthew–John

KEY POINTS

1. God came to earth in human form as Jesus by entering history through the womb of an earthly human.
2. Soon after His birth, Mary and Joseph took Jesus to the temple. There He was dedicated to God by Simeon.
3. Jesus asked John to baptize Him as an act of public identification with God.
4. Jesus taught parables—earthly stories with heavenly meaning.
5. Matthew, Mark, Luke, and John speak of Jesus' supernatural miracles. John called them "signs." These signs serve as support for His declaration that "no man comes to the Father, except through Me."
6. Jesus claimed to be the great "I Am": God, the One who is eternal, self-existent, and beyond time.
7. Jesus spent the bulk of His teaching predicting His death and resurrection.
8. After the resurrection, Jesus appeared in a real body, able to eat, talk, and be touched. He was standing before them as a live human, fully healed and resurrected.
9. Jesus gave one final challenge—to share His story with people from all faiths, beliefs, and backgrounds.

NOTES

GROUP TRACK

Jesus transformed the meaning and symbolism of the cross. Because of His death, He transformed the cross from being a symbol of torture to a symbol of love.

How have you witnessed or experienced the transforming power of Jesus Christ at work in your life or in the lives of those around you?

What do you think happens to someone when God begins to transform his or her life more and more to the image of Christ? What does that look like?

When writing about Jesus, C. S. Lewis said, "A man who was merely a man and said the sort of things Jesus said would not be a great moral teacher. ... Either this man was, and is, the Son of God, or else a madman or something worse."[1] Read these self-proclamations by Jesus found in the Gospel of John. These statements embedded a dark hatred of Jesus deep in the hearts of the Pharisees (the religious elite of Jesus' day).

> The Father and I are one.
> JOHN 10:30

> You call Me Teacher and Lord. This is well said, for I am.
> JOHN 13:13

> Jesus said to them, "I assure you: Before Abraham was, I am."
> JOHN 8:58

> Jesus said to him, "Have I been among you all this
> time without your knowing Me, Philip? The one
> who has seen Me has seen the Father."
> JOHN 14:9

What do these statements of Jesus teach us?

Why do you think these statements made the religious people so angry with Jesus?

> Jesus told him, "I am the way, the truth, and the life.
> No one comes to the Father except through Me."
> JOHN 14:6

Think about those words: *way, truth, life*. What does this verse mean to you?

John 14:6 doesn't mean that He creates a path for us to hike. Jesus hiked down into our sin, rebellion, and failures, put them on His back and climbed on a cross. His innocence for our guilt. He died in our place, for our crimes, and in turn gave us His life. In all other religions man has to work his way to God. We can never do enough, be enough to impress God. Jesus took our place. This is what it means for Jesus to be the way, the truth, the life.

Some interpret John 14:6 as a negative statement, but based on what we just read, that's a bit difficult to do. Jesus isn't just saying that there's no other way to God except through Him. Jesus is also saying that there's no one else coming for us *except* Him.

> [7] A woman of Samaria came to draw water.
> "Give Me a drink," Jesus said to her, [8] for His
> disciples had gone into town to buy food.
> [9] "How is it that You, a Jew, ask for a drink from
> me, a Samaritan woman?" she asked Him. For
> Jews do not associate with Samaritans.
> [10] Jesus answered, "If you knew the gift of God, and
> who is saying to you, 'Give Me a drink,' you would
> ask Him, and He would give you living water."

> [11] "Sir," said the woman, "You don't even have a bucket, and
> the well is deep. So where do You get this 'living water'?
> [13] Jesus said, "Everyone who drinks from this water will
> get thirsty again. [14] But whoever drinks from the water
> that I will give him will never get thirsty again—ever!
> In fact, the water I will give him will become a well of
> water springing up within him for eternal life."
> JOHN 4:7-11,13-14

Jesus and the woman at the well are talking about water when Jesus turns the exchange metaphorical. What are some of the implications of the "living water" He references?

What is this "living water" to you? What do you need it to be during this season of your life?

Much of this exchange in John 4 is about knowing (vv. 10,17-19,22,25). What do you think it means to "know" Jesus?

If you need to talk to someone about your relationship with God, ask your small-group leader or pastor at your church.

1. C. S. Lewis, *Mere Christianity*, (New York: HarperCollins, 1980), 68.

WRAP

As Christ followers our lives are supposed to be filled with joy and meaning. So why do we sometimes find ourselves struggling, feeling guilty? Why are we tired—not physically tired as much as emotionally tired, spiritually tired? We fill our lives doing good, but it never feels like enough. The answer isn't in doing more. The answer is in Matthew 11:28: "Come to Me, all of you who are weary and burdened, and I will give you rest."

And that's what God's greatest gift is all about. We are loved unconditionally. We have nothing to prove, no one to impress.

Chad talks a lot in this week's video message about our need to stop trying to measure up but instead *look up* for our forgiveness. When we try to "measure up," we become critical, judgmental, and self-righteous. But when we look up for our forgiveness and recognize how very much we've been forgiven for, we are able to accept His gift and in return love and forgive even more.

> No condemnation now exists for those in Christ Jesus.
> ROMANS 8:1

What are some ways you need to "look up"?

God, thank You for the gift of Jesus Christ. Thank You for sending Your Son to die on the cross for our sins. Thank You for paving the way back to You. Jesus, thank You for coming for us when no one else could. Amen.

▶ PERSONAL TRACK

LIKE FATHER, LIKE SON

What does your name mean? When you introduce yourself to someone, what name do you use? Does it differ depending on who you meet? Why?

In the Old Testament, when God would introduce or reveal another attribute about Himself, the nation of Israel would attach a name to it. For instance:

Jehovah-Jireh is translated "God Who Provides."

El-Elyon is translated "God Most High."

El-Olam is translated "Everlasting God."

El-Shaddai is translated "God Almighty."

Remember when God came to Moses in the form of a burning bush? He revealed His personal name to him. Wow! Imagine the God of the universe actually giving us His name.

> 14 God replied to Moses, "I AM WHO I AM. This is what you are to say to the Israelites: I AM has sent me to you." 15 God also said to Moses, "Say this to the Israelites: Yahweh, the God of your fathers, the God of Abraham, the God of Isaac, and the God of Jacob, has sent me to you. This is My name forever; this is how I am to be remembered in every generation."
>
> EXODUS 3:14-15

In what ways has God revealed Himself to you?

When Jesus walked the earth, He revealed who He was in the same tradition of His Father. He took the idea of God as "I AM" and further defined it for the people to whom He ministered. The seven "I am" statements of Jesus reveal many things about Him.

1. I am the light of the world. (John 8:12; 9:5)

2. I am the bread of life. (John 6:35)

3. I am the good shepherd. (John 10:11,14)

4. I am the door of the sheep. (John 10:7,9)

5. I am the resurrection and the life. (John 11:25)

6. I am the way, the truth, and the life. (John 14:6)

7. I am the true vine. (John 15:1)

Which of these statements means the most to you now? Why?

Who is Jesus to you? If He appeared to you right now and said, "I am the
_____," how would He fill in the blank to meet your needs?

As you continue to walk with God, you will become more like Jesus, His Son.

We all, with unveiled faces, are looking as in a mirror at the
glory of the Lord and are being transformed into the same image
from glory to glory; this is from the Lord who is the Spirit.
2 CORINTHIANS 3:18

Find one attribute you admire in Christ, and choose to focus on it for the day.
Live it out in your home and work.

*God, thank You for revealing Yourself to me. Jesus, thank You for being who You
are to me. Help me to become more like You. Amen.*

JESUS FULFILLED THE LAW

¹⁷ Don't assume that I came to destroy the Law or the Prophets.
I did not come to destroy but to fulfill. ¹⁸ For I assure you: Until
heaven and earth pass away, not the smallest letter or one stroke
of a letter will pass from the law until all things are accomplished.
MATTHEW 5:17-18

We have just fast tracked our way through the Old Testament, also known as the Law and the Prophets. You know a little about the old covenant, the sacrificial system, and how the nation of Israel tried to live by this Law from the beginning of their relationship with God. They failed often, as you have seen, but the Law was given for a purpose.

God revealed it to them for two reasons: (1) so His people would be a different kind of people to the world, and (2) so they would know that they were completely unable to keep the Law.

It seems counterproductive at first, but the Law served as a constant reminder to those trying to keep that Law that they couldn't do it. It was God's way of reminding every individual that they needed a Savior. No matter how many sacrifices, rituals, or celebrations, they always had to keep making more. It was stifling, and everyone under the Law knew just how sinful they really were.

In what ways do you identify with those who are constantly trying to keep the Law?

How have you most recently been reminded that you need a Savior?

Another way that Jesus is the greatest gift is His relationship to the Law. He literally fulfilled the Law by living a perfect life. He never sinned. He never violated a commandment. He was perfect. Think of it in terms of a contract, like a home mortgage or lease. The contract specifies the requirements from both parties. Only when all the conditions are met is the contract fulfilled. This is what Jesus did for mankind.

He fulfilled both sides of the contract—for all of humanity He lived a perfect life; for God He died on the cross as the perfect sacrifice for sin.

Jesus also fulfilled the Law spiritually. He knew the purpose behind the Law and revealed it in how He lived His life on earth. Jesus raised the standard in that He bypassed the required conditions of obedience and went straight to the spiritual.

Read Matthew 5:17-48 sometime this week. Notice how many times Jesus says, "You have heard that it was said, … but I tell you …" In each example, Jesus is quoting the Law and explaining not just the letter of the Law, but the spirit behind the Law.

There is a lot of freedom in God's gift of grace. Does that feel freeing or frightening to you? Explain.

Romans 6:1-2 says, "Should we continue in sin so that grace may multiply? Absolutely not!" Grace is not freedom to do as we please, it's freedom to be everything God dreamed we could be.

How can you know if you are taking advantage of this gift of grace? How can you make it right?

God, help me to live by the spirit of the Law. Remind me every day that I need You. Amen.

JESUS PAVES THE WAY TO GOD

"We on this continent should never forget that men
first crossed the Atlantic not to find soil for their
ploughs but to secure liberty for their souls."
ROBERT J. MCCRACKEN

When Jesus lived on this earth, He was blazing a trail back to God. He said, "I am the way, the truth, and the life. No one comes to the Father except through Me" (John 14:6). Paving a road is hard work. But paving the path back to God, now that requires some sacrifice.

To keep this road clear, Jesus spoke out many times against those who distorted the Truth. He called them dogs, snakes, blind guides, whitewashed tombs. They looked holy and acted righteous, yet they were leading people down the wrong path. Part of what Jesus came to do was show people the right path.

> 7 Keep asking, and it will be given to you. Keep searching, and you will find. Keep knocking, and the door will be opened to you. 8 For everyone who asks receives, and the one who searches finds, and to the one who knocks, the door will be opened. 9 What man among you, if his son asks him for bread, will give him a stone? 10 Or if he asks for a fish, will give him a snake? 11 If you then, who are evil, know how to give good gifts to your children, how much more will your Father in heaven give good things to those who ask Him! 12 Therefore, whatever you want others to do for you, do also the same for them—this is the Law and the Prophets. 13 Enter through the narrow gate. For the gate is wide and the road is broad that leads to destruction, and there are many who go through it. 14 How narrow is the gate and difficult the road that leads to life, and few find it.
>
> MATTHEW 7:7-14

Watch out for false prophets. Watch out for false doctrine. Watch out for false disciples. Jesus was constantly warning those who would have the ears to hear Him. Jesus is lovingly and painstakingly paving the way back to God. He is giving us every signal, every sign, every opportunity to see the path and stay on it.

When we listen to others or follow others down a different path, it's like going the wrong way down a one-way street. It's like trying to navigate through a large crowd that is moving in the other direction. It's like endlessly going up an escalator that's going down. It will wear us out.

Have you ever veered off the road to God? How did you get back on it?

Jesus knows the way—He is the way. And He was calling people to lead a different kind of life. He knew it would be in stark contrast to what they had always known—relational instead of religious. His way was not the way that the crowd was traveling. It was a different road altogether.

What other paths have you been on? How did you come to discover that Jesus was the way?

Imagine being responsible for paving the way not with roads for wheels, but with freedom for souls. What actions do you think that would require of you?

God, show me the way I need to go every day. Keep me on the straight and narrow. I want to follow You for the rest of my life. Amen.

JESUS GAVE HIS LIFE

Like most people, you likely have a résumé. On this résumé, you list your education, experience, information about where you live, and any accomplishments pertinent to the position for which you are applying. Imagine if Jesus had a résumé.

Education: Home School

Background/Experience: Builder, Religious dissenter.

Accomplishments:
Three years in ministry. Proven track record for developing leaders.
Persecuted for telling the truth. Crucified. Died. Rose again. Defeated sin and death.

Current location: Seated at the right hand of God. Interceding for all mankind.

How would your résumé read as a follower of Christ?

Think for a moment how unqualified each and every one of us is to fill the position Jesus had to fill. Whoever was going to give his life to save mankind, he had to be perfect.

²³ For all have sinned and fall short of the glory of God.
²⁴ They are justified freely by His grace through the redemption that is in Christ Jesus. ²⁵ God presented Him as a propitiation through faith in His blood, to demonstrate His righteousness, because in His restraint God passed over the sins previously committed. ²⁶ God presented Him to demonstrate His righteousness at the present time, so that He would be righteous and declare righteous the one who has faith in Jesus.
ROMANS 3:23-26

Jesus became God's demonstration of love for the world to see.

Jesus became God's way to save all mankind.

Jesus died to reconciled God and man.

Jesus became God's declaration that He was a just God.

Jesus became all of this because He was the only One qualified to give His life.

How are you spending your life in response to the gift Jesus gave—the gift of Himself?

In what ways does your life demonstrate your belief that Christ really died for you?

It is no surprise, knowing what we know about God, that He would give the best gift. We have seen Him pursue humanity from the very beginning. God has never held out on us. He has given Himself, His Son, His Spirit, and His Word.

> [16] Don't be deceived, my dearly loved brothers. [17] Every generous act and every perfect gift is from above, coming down from the Father of lights; with Him there is no variation or shadow cast by turning.
>
> JAMES 1:16-17

Spend a few moments thinking and meditating on Jesus. Let this time set the course for your day.

God, help me see when the Enemy tries to embed lies in my heart. Remind me of how good and great You are. Amen.

JESUS SENDS THE HOLY SPIRIT

During His time on earth, Jesus taught many things and His audience varied. Sometimes the crowds would show up. Sometimes His teaching was limited to His disciples.

Much of what Jesus taught was not understood by any of them, and sometimes Jesus would say things to a crowd, then explain further to the disciples when they were alone together.

One of the most important teachings, and often one of the most controversial, is Jesus' words concerning the Holy Spirit. The Holy Spirit is a part of the Trinity, and Jesus said in John 14 that He would be leaving, but the Father would send someone else in His place—the Holy Spirit.

Jesus was crucified during the Passover and resurrected on the day of the celebration of First Fruits. After that, He remained on the earth for 40 days, and then He was taken up into heaven. In Acts 1 Jesus told the disciples that they should remain in Jerusalem to wait for the Father's promise, the Holy Spirit. About 10 days later, during the Feast of Weeks (Pentecost), the Spirit was sent from heaven.

At this time, the disciples were filled with the Spirit and empowered to do many great and wonderful things. The purpose of the filling of the Spirit was to fulfill the promise Jesus made that they would do even greater things than He did.

> [12] I assure you: The one who believes in Me will also do the works that I do. And he will do even greater works than these, because I am going to the Father. [13] Whatever you ask in My name, I will do it so that the Father may be glorified in the Son. [14] If you ask Me anything in My name, I will do it. [15] If you love Me, you will keep My commands. [16] And I will ask the Father, and He will give you another Counselor to be with you forever. [17] He is the Spirit of truth. The world is unable to receive Him because it doesn't see Him or know Him. But you do know Him, because He remains with you and will be in you.
>
> JOHN 14:12-17

Do you think the promise of God is still valid for us today? Can we be filled with the Spirit and do great things for God? Explain.

If you could do something great for God, and you knew you could only accomplish it in the power of God, what would it be?

The Holy Spirit has been active in the affairs of mankind since the very beginning. He was present when the world was created. But His very special work is here and now within the lives of the believer.

He convicts the world of their sin.

He brings back those who are separated from God.

He intercedes and prays to God on the believer's behalf.

He works to set apart the believer to make him like Christ.

He guides and helps the believer in making disciples of Christ.

He comforts and empowers when the believer experiences persecution and hard times.

Do you rely on the Holy Spirit as much as you should? In which of the areas listed above do you need to engage the Holy Spirit more?

Holy Spirit, help me trust You more. Show me how I can rely upon You not just for the big things in life, but in the everyday things, too. Amen.

Fast Track

Session 7

THE CHURCH: A NEW MISSION

ACTS–THESSALONIANS

ACTS–THESSALONIANS

"Do not go where the path may lead, go instead
where there is no path and leave a trail."
RALPH WALDO EMERSON

From the pages of the Old Testament to the pages of the

New Testament, Scripture records how God has revealed

Himself in the hearts and lives and affairs of mankind.

Each chapter chronicles the activity of God and man.

The stories remind us of God's heart for all mankind—that there's always been a plan for the redemption of man. There has always been provision to save His people. In the Old Testament the plan may have been shrouded in a mystery or a prophecy. But in the New Testament the plan is out in the open, on full display. Jesus Christ is the mystery unveiled. The plan for redemption is in full effect.

Saint Augustine said, "The world is a book, and those who do not travel read only one page." The church isn't a book, but it does have a story. It begins in the Book of Acts, and it continues to be written today. Some chapters of the church's history are dark and bleak, while others are filled with hope and inspiration. Jesus is the ultimate in God's revelation, purpose, story, and love for all of us. And our surrendered response to Jesus is how He builds the church.

The church's mission is to continue the work of Christ. As ambassadors of God to a broken and busted world, we are called to participate with God. The church and its mission are the way God works through us in life and purpose. Our passion to know God and follow Christ will display compassion for the world.

As your story intersects with God's, what new story are you writing together?

BACK TRACK

In one of your daily readings this past week, you learned how Jesus came to fulfill the Law and not abolish it. As a result, there is freedom in Christ that is found in no other religion. How do you deal with that freedom? Have you had to make any adjustments? Explain your response to your group.

FRAMING THE STORY

Real life adventures can be exciting and dangerous, grueling and death-defying. Upon which of these adventures would you have enjoyed embarking the most? Why?

Lewis and Clark's expedition across the American frontier
NASA's Apollo Space Mission(s) to space/the moon
Sally Ride's journey as the first American woman in space
Marco Polo's adventures throughout the eastern world
Lieutenant Isaac Strain's exploration of Panama's isthmus
	(for the Panama Canal)
Henry Morton Stanley's journey through the African Congo
Anne Bradstreet's work as the first woman writer to be published in America
Martin Luther King, Jr.'s work with civil rights
Shirley Chisholm's journey to run for President of the United States
Other: _____

VIDEO TRACK

Acts–Thessalonians

KEY POINTS

1. Jesus went up, He sent the Holy Spirit down, and the disciples went out to deliver a unique message unlike any religion, philosophy, or teaching.
2. The Holy Spirit appeared as a fire to remind Christ-followers that His Spirit would be burning inside them now.
3. There is a gulf between us and our Creator. Religion is about mankind trying to get to God. The gospel is about God coming to us.
4. The early Christ followers took their personal income and private property and chose to give it away to others in need.
5. Stephen became a significant force in the early church. He preached the new message of Jesus, and he was stoned to death as a result.
6. Saul was shocked to learn he had been persecuting the very God he was working so hard to impress. Jesus restored Saul's sight, changed his name to Paul, and commissioned him to deliver the message of Christ.
7. Paul circled the known world three times. He invited anyone he met to explore the message of Christ.
8. Paul knew that if he could transform a leader, a ruler, or a king, the entire countryside could be transformed.
9. Paul was placed on a ship bound for Rome and Caesar. When the ship hit severe storms, Paul continued to share the message of Christ.

NOTES

GROUP TRACK

Which of the following events or individuals are most memorable (or most unbelievable) to you?

Jesus Christ as He ascended into heaven
Pentecost when the Holy Spirit first came to earth to dwell inside believers
Peter when he spoke with a tongue of fire
The generosity that poured out from the believers when the church was born
Stephen who gave up his life for the gospel
Ananias and Sapphira who said they gave everything but lied
Paul's conversion experience on the road to Damascus

How do you think each of these stories serve as a God-given reminder about the importance of our mission with God on this earth?

Think about this for a moment. This new mission—given only to the church—is God's plan to reach and save the world. No other people group or entity has been commissioned by God to represent Him to a lost world and spread His message of hope.

> Just think—you don't need a thing, you've got it all! All God's gifts are right in front of you as you wait expectantly for our Master Jesus to arrive on the scene for the Finale. And not only that, but God himself is right alongside to keep you steady and on track until things are all wrapped up by Jesus. God, who got you started in this spiritual adventure, shares with us the life of his Son and our Master Jesus. He will never give up on you. Never forget that.
> 1 CORINTHIANS 1:7-9, MSG

Why do you think it would be important for Paul—the writer in this case—to stress that God will never give up on you?

In Framing the Story we talked about different adventures. How does your relationship with God on mission compare to those adventures? How do you think it should?

> [41] So those who accepted his message were baptized, and that day about 3,000 people were added to them. [42] And they devoted themselves to the apostles' teaching, to the fellowship, to the breaking of bread, and to the prayers. [44] Now all the believers were together and held all things in common. [45] They sold their possessions and property and distributed the proceeds to all, as anyone had a need. [46] Every day they devoted themselves to meeting together in the temple complex, and broke bread from house to house. They ate their food with a joyful and humble attitude, [47] praising God and having favor with all the people. And every day the Lord added to them those who were being saved.
> ACTS 2:41-42,44-47

Discuss your experience with church life over the years. What words describe it best?

Read Acts 2:41-42 and 44-47. Why do you think this would be the first official act of obedience within this community of believers?

What is standing between you and a life more in line with the way the disciples were living according to these verses in Acts?

The instinctive generosity that poured out from all the believers was simply amazing. Unprompted and unscripted, this was just a pure and simple expression of gratitude to God for what He had done in their lives.

When we see the church in action, it solidifies the idea that being on mission with God means adapting a generous lifestyle toward others. Generously living for God is generously giving to others. Look how Paul expressed this concept later in the life of the church.

> [6] Remember this: The person who sows sparingly will also reap sparingly, and the person who sows generously will also reap generously. [7] Each person should do as he has decided in his heart—not reluctantly or out of necessity, for God loves a cheerful giver. [8] And God is able to make every grace overflow to you, so that in every way, always having everything you need, you may excel in every good work.
> 2 CORINTHIANS 9:6-8

Break into groups of 2-3 and make a list of what you think it means to be a cheerful giver. Talk about who is impacted and how. Then come back together and share some of your answers with the large group.

How does the promise from God at the end of that passage encourage you to move forward with a generous lifestyle for God? What mission would you like to be a part of in sharing the gospel?

What kind of church would your church be if everyone was just like you? Would it be a giving church? A growing church? A church that loves at all costs? A church that shares the gospel? A compassionate church? A church on mission?

If money wasn't an issue, what is one thing you wish or dream you and your church could be a part of on mission with God?

WRAP

Life with God is an "aggressive cooperation" with Him. He wants to be with us, and He wants to do life with us. That means finding where God is moving and working to accomplish our mission together.

One of the greatest tools you have for changing the world is your story. What's your story? What has God done in your life? What is He doing right now? Ask God to show you where you can use your story to impact the lives of others. Through your story you are uniquely qualified to reach people for Christ—in ways no one else can.

Don't think short-term or long-term missions. Think living missionally. Accomplishing a task, sharing the gospel, sharing resources—all of these activities for God are just part of our everyday lives.

If we begin to move in this direction and think in these terms, there's no telling where God might call us to experience His adventure!

God, show us what You want us to do for You. We want to be on mission for You. Give us clear direction as we move forward on our spiritual adventure. Give us comfort, joy, and Your peace as we follow You wherever You want us to go. Amen.

PERSONAL TRACK

PENTECOST

What is now referred to as Pentecost (the Greek word for "50th day") was originally called the Feast of Weeks, or Shavuot. It is a Jewish festival commemorating the 50th day after Passover. That was the day that God gave the Law to the people of Israel from Mount Sinai. The Jews celebrated Passover for 7 weeks, that's 49 days. And on the 50th day, they celebrated Shavuot.

These holy days are still celebrated by practicing Jews, but they have come to be known for something completely different to Christians all over the world. Passover corresponds to the day Jesus was crucified, so for Christ followers, the 50th day is Pentecost.

[1] When the day of Pentecost had arrived, they were all together in one place. [2] Suddenly a sound like that of a violent rushing wind came from heaven, and it filled the whole house where they were staying. [3] And tongues, like flames of fire that were divided, appeared to them and rested on each one of them. [4] Then they were all filled with the Holy Spirit and began to speak in different languages, as the Spirit gave them ability for speech. [5] There were Jews living in Jerusalem, devout men from every nation under heaven. [6] When this sound occurred, a crowd came together and was confused because each one heard them speaking in his own language. [12] They were all astounded and perplexed, saying to one another, "What could this be?" [13] But some sneered and said, "They're full of new wine!" [14] But Peter stood up with the Eleven, raised his voice, and proclaimed to them: "Men of Judah and all you residents of Jerusalem, let me explain this to you and pay attention to my words. [15] For these people are not drunk, as you suppose, since it's only nine in the morning. [16] On the contrary, this is what was spoken through the prophet Joel: [17] And it will be in the last days, says God, that I will pour out My Spirit on all humanity; then your sons and your daughters will prophesy, your young men will see visions, and your old men will dream dreams.

The Church: A New Mission

on My male and female slaves in those days,
and they will prophesy.
ACTS 2:1-6,12-18

When was the last time you were in awe of what the Spirit was doing in your
life and/or in the lives of those around you? What was He doing?

This outpouring of the Spirit was the beginning of something new. Everything that
Jesus taught was coming to pass. A new church was beginning, a new way of doing
things, a new way of relating to God.

Tell of a time when the Spirit worked through you to build the kingdom of God.
What was it like?

Read the Book of Acts. You will see mighty works of the Spirit and the church. People
were saved, healed, set free, and called by God to do even more wonderful works for
Him. The Spirit who shook up the Shavuot and gave birth to the church is the same
Spirit dwelling with you right now. We may not stand before a crowd of people from
different nations, speak so they hear in their own language, or possess the healing
touch, but the Spirit still empowers people to be witnesses. He desires for us to do
good and mighty works to this very day.

You receive this same Spirit when you become a Christian. Everything God has to
give you is given in that moment when you accept Christ. Now the task is to go—tell
everyone what God has done for you!

---

*God, help me contribute to Your kingdom work in ways You see fit. I want to be used by
You. Amen.*

PAUL'S JOURNEYS

> [24] Five times I received 39 lashes from Jews.
> [25] Three times I was beaten with rods by the Romans.
> Once I was stoned by my enemies.
> Three times I was shipwrecked.
> I have spent a night and a day
> in the open sea.
> [26] On frequent journeys, I faced
> dangers from rivers,
> dangers from robbers,
> dangers from my own people,
> dangers from the Gentiles,
> dangers in the city,
> dangers in the open country,
> dangers on the sea,
> and dangers among false brothers.
> 2 CORINTHIANS 11:24-26

Think about the adventures you have been on for Christ. What was one you considered fun? One you considered difficult?

How much would you be willing to endure to be on mission for and with God? Answer honestly.

The apostle Paul was arguably the most prolific missionary of all time. Look at what he accomplished in a few short decades:

1. Paul completed three missionary journeys around the Mediterranean Sea (this was the known world at that time). He was literally going to follow Christ's command to "Go into all the world and preach the gospel to the whole creation" (Mark 16:15).

2. Paul wrote 13 of the 27 books (about half of the content) in the New Testament.

3. Paul planted at least 14 churches (possibly as many as 20).

4. Paul trained church leaders in every city to shepherd the new church plants.

The Book of Acts is as much about the early church as it is about Paul's calling and work. Before he was Paul, he was known as Saul, a persecutor of Christians. His old way of life had a lot to offer him. He was rising fast in the ranks of the religious elite. But something changed inside him.

> 4 If anyone else thinks he has grounds for confidence in the flesh, I have more: 5 circumcised the eighth day; of the nation of Israel, of the tribe of Benjamin, a Hebrew born of Hebrews; regarding the law, a Pharisee; 6 regarding zeal, persecuting the church; regarding the righteousness that is in the law, blameless. 7 But everything that was a gain to me, I have considered to be a loss because of Christ. 8 More than that, I also consider everything to be a loss in view of the surpassing value of knowing Christ Jesus my Lord. Because of Him I have suffered the loss of all things and consider them filth, so that I may gain Christ 9 and be found in Him, not having a righteousness of my own from the law, but one that is through faith in Christ—the righteousness from God based on faith. 10 My goal is to know Him and the power of His resurrection and the fellowship of His sufferings, being conformed to His death. 12 Not that I have already reached the goal or am already fully mature, but I make every effort to take hold of it because I also have been taken hold of by Christ Jesus. 14 I pursue as my goal the prize promised by God's heavenly call in Christ Jesus.
>
> PHILIPPIANS 3:4-10,12,14

Paul's change on the inside matches his journey on the outside—radical and restless. How has God changed you? Was there ever a time you were radical and restless for Christ?

God, help me see the value of Your mission in my life. Give me the strength to continue in the face of hardship and adversity. Amen.

THE CORINTHIAN CHURCH

Paul planted the church in Corinth on his second missionary journey. He traveled to Corinth from Athens and met Priscilla and Aquila there. They went into business together making tents for a living, and Paul taught in a synagogue until tension with certain Jews made him seek an alternative location.

Corinth was a wealthy city. It was a center of trade for the Roman empire and had two sea ports. It was also a large city, with a population of approximately half a million people. And Corinth was a very immoral city. At one point Corinth had a temple to the goddess Aphrodite with a thousand prostitutes. Because of all these factors, Corinth was a challenging location to start a church. And once the church was planted, it was a challenge for Paul to keep its members on track.

> Have you ever been distracted in your faith? What took your attention away from God?

> How did you get back on track?

Paul visited the Corinthian church several times and wrote several letters, two of which are in the Bible. After Paul left Corinth and began his third journey, he got word from some members of the church that there were disagreements on vital topics and doctrinal issues that needed to be sorted out. He had already written the church a letter, speaking against association with immoral people. But with the new issues that arose, Paul felt he needed to go to Corinth and address them in person.

Just reading the first letter to the Corinthian church, we can easily observe they were having issues. Paul addressed factions in the church and how to avoid them. They misunderstood the nature of the gospel. They dealt with pride and lawsuits, sexual sin and marriage issues. They needed instruction for living single (or single again) and for married couples, too. They were abusing the Lord's Supper. This Corinthian church was a mess! Even though Paul confronted these issues head-on with strong words, he penned the most definitive passages on true, everlasting, enduring love.

3 And if I donate all my goods to feed the poor,
and if I give my body in order to boast
but do not have love, I gain nothing.
4 Love is patient, love is kind.
Love does not envy,
is not boastful, is not conceited,
5 does not act improperly,
is not selfish, is not provoked,
and does not keep a record of wrongs.
6 Love finds no joy in unrighteousness
but rejoices in the truth.
7 It bears all things, believes all things,
hopes all things, endures all things.
8 Love never ends.
But as for prophecies,
they will come to an end;
as for languages, they will cease;
as for knowledge, it will come to an end.
13 Now these three remain:
faith, hope, and love.
But the greatest of these is love.
1 CORINTHIANS 13:3-8,13

How does the love described here compare to how love is typically defined in our culture today?

Love as defined here by Paul wants the best for others. What typically motivates your love for others?

Love is a priority, but it is also a pursuit.

Help me, God, to see where I am most distracted from Your kingdom work. Give me the courage to love others like You want me to love.

THE THESSALONIAN CHURCH

Thessalonica was another seaport city in the Roman Empire. A wealthy, large city, they suffered from some of the same corruption found in other cities Paul visited. He helped start the church in Thessalonica during his second missionary journey. He was only there for about three weeks, but during this time he saw many Gentiles come to know the Lord, and a few Jews as well. He was also able to teach the new Christians much concerning their new lives as followers of Christ.

Paul left Thessalonica and went to Corinth. While he was there, he received word from Timothy that the new believers in Thessalonica had grown much in faith and love, but they needed additional direction from Paul in several matters.

One aspect of Paul's teaching was on the imminent return of Christ. It seems from Paul's letters to the Thessalonians that the church keyed in on this teaching above any other. Paul seemed to have believed it was possible for Christ to return in his life-time. But he also knew that no person would know for sure when Christ would return.

> [13] We do not want you to be uninformed, brothers, concerning those who are asleep, so that you will not grieve like the rest, who have no hope. [14] Since we believe that Jesus died and rose again, in the same way God will bring with Him those who have fallen asleep through Jesus. [15] For we say this to you by a revelation from the Lord: We who are still alive at the Lord's coming will certainly have no advantage over those who have fallen asleep. [16] For the Lord Himself will descend from heaven with a shout, with the archangel's voice, and with the trumpet of God, and the dead in Christ will rise first. [17] Then we who are still alive will be caught up together with them in the clouds to meet the Lord in the air and so we will always be with the Lord. [18] Therefore encourage one another with these words.
>
> 1 THESSALONIANS 4:13-18

At one time the Thessalonians were hardworking and eager to share what they had learned, but after Paul left some of them became so convinced that Christ was returning soon that they gave up their jobs and were just sitting around waiting for Jesus to come back. Their beliefs had driven them to the point of paralysis.

Paul encouraged them to keep working hard so they could win the respect of others and not have to depend on anyone for their daily needs. Unfortunately, they did not take these words to heart. Not long later, Paul had to write Thessalonica a second letter on the same topic.

> How do you process your beliefs about God? Is it balanced? Do you camp out on one topic more than any other? Why?

> In your opinion, how are you to live out your life while you wait for Jesus to return? Be specific.

Paul made it clear that the Lord would return again, but since nobody knows when that will be, we should all continue to live lives of great Christian character. The result will be many more entering the kingdom when Christ returns.

The message here is not to stop everything and wait for Jesus to come back. The message is one of hope, resting in the knowledge that we may not know *when* Jesus is coming back but we *do* know He's coming for us. Our lives here are only temporary. Our Hope is eternal.

God, teach me what's most important, and show me how to apply Your Word to my life and live it out until Jesus returns. Amen.

PAUL AND TIMOTHY

Who has been a spiritual father (or mother) to you? How did this person earn this role in your life? How do you respond to direction from this person?

Timothy was Paul's son in the faith. Timothy knew the heart and mind of Paul, perhaps better than anyone else. Paul states that he and Timothy were like-minded, especially concerning the welfare of the church in Philippi.

Timothy accompanied Paul on his second missionary journey. During this time, Paul decided that there was no one like Timothy.

> [19] I hope in the Lord Jesus to send Timothy to you soon so that I also may be encouraged when I hear news about you. [20] For I have no one else like-minded who will genuinely care about your interests; [21] all seek their own interests, not those of Jesus Christ. [22] But you know his proven character, because he has served with me in the gospel ministry like a son with a father.
> PHILIPPIANS 2:19-22

After all the time they spent together in their travels, Paul knew that Timothy was the right person to stay behind and shepherd the church in Ephesus. Timothy was young, but Paul knew he would be exactly who the Ephesians needed as a pastor. Ephesus was a key city—Paul knew that if they could evangelize this area, many other cities would open up to the gospel. It was a great responsibility that he entrusted to Timothy, and Timothy didn't let Paul down.

> [11] Command and teach these things. [12] Let no one despise your youth; instead, you should be an example to the believers in speech, in conduct, in love, in faith, in purity. [13] Until I come, give your attention to public reading, exhortation, and teaching. [14] Do not neglect the gift that is in you; it was given to you through prophecy, with the laying on of hands by the council of elders. [15] Practice these things; be committed to them, so that your progress may be evident to all.
> 1 TIMOTHY 4:11-15

Paul never stopped encouraging Timothy. Even when Paul was probably aware that his life would be coming to an end very soon, he encouraged Timothy to not be timid in his faith. Rather, he should remain bold.

> [12] All those who want to live a godly life in Christ Jesus will be persecuted. [13] Evil people and impostors will become worse, deceiving and being deceived. [14] But as for you, continue in what you have learned and firmly believed. You know those who taught you, [15] and you know that from childhood you have known the sacred Scriptures, which are able to give you wisdom for salvation through faith in Christ Jesus.
>
> 2 TIMOTHY 3:12-15

Paul had been a mentor to Timothy and in return Timothy made Paul proud, much like a father is with his children. Is there someone in your life who looks up to you? You have great influence on this person, either for good or for bad, just by the way you act around him or her or the way you include this person in what you are doing. Be a good role model and leave a legacy of being a great leader.

Who are you investing in and discipling? What can you learn from the relationship between Paul and Timothy about how to encourage that person or build a relationship with him or her?

God, guide me to help teach the next generation of Christ followers. They need to know You. Show me how to encourage them for Your sake. Amen.

THE END: NEVER GIVE UP

REVELATION, DANIEL, MATTHEW 24

REVELATION, DANIEL, MATTHEW 24

"For even the very wise cannot see all ends."
J. R. R. TOLKIEN, IN *THE FELLOWSHIP OF THE RING*

Some Old and New Testament prophecies have been fulfilled. Others are still to come. What is amazing is that some people dismiss the pending prophecies as myth or superstition despite all the evidence that fulfilled prophecies in Scripture have brought.

Friedrich von Schlegel said, "The historian is a prophet facing backwards." A similar sentiment we all have expressed is, "Hindsight is 20/20." We may look back on an event with a sense of regret and wish we could have seen it coming. We become the prophet facing backward when we connect the dots of past events.

Concerning the end times, we don't know what day it's all going to end. We don't know the details on how it's all going to end. We don't know what time it's all going to end. All we know is that it's definitely going to end.

> [26] This is the plan prepared
> for the whole earth,
> and this is the hand stretched out
> against all the nations.
> [27] The LORD of Hosts Himself has planned it;
> therefore, who can stand in its way?
> It is His hand that is outstretched,
> so who can turn it back?
> ISAIAH 14:26-27

Let this concluding session bolster your faith in God's Word. Let it strengthen your resolve to follow Jesus to the very end, whenever that may be. May there be clarity where there's been confusion. The one thing we want to avoid is looking back with a sense of regret and saying, "I wish I would have seen this coming." There's no need for hindsight. The dots have already been connected. Follow Jesus by faith.

BACK TRACK

Your personal study this past week focused on God's mission for your life. How are you partnering with the Holy Spirit in this endeavor? Have you changed the way you love others? The way you invest in others? Discuss this with the group.

FRAMING THE STORY

Think about all the movies, books, TV shows, or stories over the past years that portray the future. In your opinion, what makes a futuristic story really good and creative?

If Jesus doesn't come back sooner, what do you think our world will look like in 50 years? 100 years?

VIDEO TRACK

Revelation, Daniel, Matthew 24

KEY POINTS

1. John writes letters to seven churches, passing along Jesus' reminders to examine their hearts and check that God is still their first love and priority.
2. John received a vivid vision from Jesus during a difficult time in his life when he, like other disciples, was imprisoned. Despite his familiarity with the earthly Jesus, he was stunned to see Christ in His full, powerful majesty.
3. Jesus begins the vision with a picture of the rapture. God reaches down from heaven to personally escort His followers to heaven.
4. The rapture concludes, leaving no one on earth who trusted Christ as a forgiver and leader. God gave a seven-year object lesson to reveal mankind's need for Jesus as Rescuer and King.
5. The stunned world had to choose which resurrected king was the real One: The Christ of the past or the Anti-Christ of the present.
6. Jesus rescued Israel from an impending massacre. He wiped out the evil forces, serving as a "shield of faith" for those who called out to Him. He was the "sword" that fights against corruption.
7. Jesus sets up a literal, physical kingdom on earth for 1000 years. This is the fulfillment of a promise, or covenant, made to King David years before.
8. "Since you rejected Me as your forgiver, I'll give you what you wanted: fairness."
9. God answered the prayers of those who wanted His forgiveness. Jesus makes a new heaven and new earth, fully cleansed and renewed.

NOTES

GROUP TRACK

What part of this week's video message was new to you? How does it compare to what you have previously been taught?

What part is most concerning for you? Most comforting? Explain.

People have been wrongly predicting the future for centuries. As long as there are false prophets, there will be false prophecies. The distinctive attribute that separates biblical prophecy and all other apocalyptic literary works is that prophecy found in Scripture is true. We can go to the last chapter of the book and know how it is going to end. We may not know the specifics, but we know Who wins.

When Jesus walked the earth, even He didn't know when He was going to come back.

> [36] Now concerning that day and hour no one knows—neither the angels in heaven, nor the Son—except the Father only. [37] As the days of Noah were, so the coming of the Son of Man will be. [38] For in those days before the flood they were eating and drinking, marrying and giving in marriage, until the day Noah boarded the ark. [39] They didn't know until the flood came and swept them all away. So this is the way the coming of the Son of Man will be: [42] Therefore be alert, since you don't know what day your Lord is coming. [43] But know this: If the homeowner had known what time the thief was coming, he would have stayed alert and not let his house be broken into. [44] This is why you also must be ready, because the Son of Man is coming at an hour you do not expect.
> MATTHEW 24:36-39,42-44

How do you think Jesus' disciples initially received and interpreted this teaching?

What do you think it means, practically, to be ready for Jesus' return if we don't know when He is coming?

The passage from Matthew 24 calls for readiness without telling us how to get ready. A clear answer can be found a little further on.

> 35 "For I was hungry
> and you gave Me something to eat;
> I was thirsty
> and you gave Me something to drink;
> I was a stranger and you took Me in;
> 36 I was naked and you clothed Me;
> I was sick and you took care of Me;
> I was in prison and you visited Me.'
> 37 Then the righteous will answer Him, "Lord, when did
> we see You hungry and feed You, or thirsty and give You
> something to drink?
> 38 When did we see You a stranger and take You in, or
> without clothes and clothe You?
> 39 When did we see You sick, or in prison, and visit You?"
> 40 And the King will answer them, "I assure
> you: Whatever you did for one of the least of
> these brothers of Mine, you did for Me."
> MATTHEW 25:35-40

We don't necessarily have to be prisoners to know what being captive might feel like. In what others ways could the needs mentioned in verses 35-36 manifest themselves in our lives or the lives of others?

When have you experienced one or more of these needs and had someone reach out to you? In what ways did that impact your desire to reach out and help others?

To which of these needs do you find yourself giving most comfortably? Which is most difficult? Explain why you think that is.

Jesus said that no one knows when He is coming back. But how would you change the way you live today if you knew for a fact Jesus would return next month or next year? How would that affect your priorities or the way you spend your time and money?

Being sheep of the Shepherd isn't about us. It's about following His lead and loving others as He loves us.

WRAP

The material we studied today explains what will happen at the end of time. These three sections of the Bible were not written to scare us, but to give us hope. The Bible explains the end of time so those who are doubtful, hurting, or fearful can find hope, healing, and comfort. Knowing the final chapter of history alleviates stress and fear today.

When we know God will be a fair judge to all, we can stop holding grudges. When we know God will reward us for every act of obedience, we can stay faithful. When we can trust God to transform the manure of life into fertilizer for new growth, we can be armed with unshakable confidence. When we know that our eternity is secured, we can view this life as temporal. When we realize that this world is broken, we're no longer surprised by trouble and pain. When we believe He can return at any moment, we are motivated to live a pure, faithful, and generous life. We can have hope today when we know what happens tomorrow.

So, who do you say He is? Fairness or forgiveness—which do you choose?

Take a moment to reflect on your entire *Fast Track* experience and finish your group time by discussing how you would complete these statements:

My favorite session was _____. (Share why.)

Something new I learned from studying *Fast Track* was _____.

For me, a difficult concept or truth to apply from the Bible is _____.

An aspect of the Bible that I'd like to explore more is _____.

God, thank You for Your Word of truth. Thank You for promising us a life with You forever. Keep us vigilant for Your Son's return. Help us to listen to the Holy Spirit who guides us by Your truth. Help us to help others along the way, and give us Your wisdom and discernment until the very end. We love You, God. Amen.

PERSONAL TRACK

THE SEVEN CHURCHES

[4] To the seven churches in Asia.

Grace and peace to you from the One who is, who was, and
who is coming; from the seven spirits before His throne;
[5] and from Jesus Christ, the faithful witness, the firstborn
from the dead and the ruler of the kings of the earth.

To Him who loves us and has set us free from our sins by His
blood, [6] and made us a kingdom, priests to His God and Father—
the glory and dominion are His forever and ever. Amen.

[7] Look! He is coming with the clouds,
and every eye will see Him,
including those who pierced Him.
And all the families of the earth
will mourn over Him.
This is certain. Amen.

[8] "I am the Alpha and the Omega," says the Lord God, "the
One who is, who was, and who is coming, the Almighty."
REVELATION 1:4-8

John wrote Revelation while in exile on the island of Patmos, and he addressed it to the seven churches in Asia. As he begins writing, Jesus speaks to each church through John—words of warning, commendation, and condemnation. The seven letters to the seven churches can be read in Revelation 2 and 3. Each letter is brief and to the point.

In the letter to Ephesus Jesus commends the church for being faithful in a few things, but rebukes them for leaving their first love. They were focused on doing the work of God and not focused on God Himself. He told them to return to their first love or risk losing everything.

The church of Smyrna was a church under persecution. Jesus exhorted them to stand firm, and He stated that He knew what they were going through and that they would continue to suffer but the reward would be great.

To the church of Pergamum, Jesus said that their city was Satan's throne, but they stood firm and held onto the name of Christ even while persecuted. However, they were allowing immorality to creep in—they were beginning to compromise. They were called to repentance and assured a special reward for being obedient.

The church in Thyatira had many good works, and they were complimented for this, but they had allowed themselves to be held under the teaching of a false prophetess who was leading them away from the Lord and into immorality.

Sardis was a church that was already dead. Its past works gave the church a reputation of being alive, but their present actions showed them to be stagnant and attempting to live off their former glory.

The church of Philadelphia was characterized as having limited strength, but even so, they were able to endure much and hold fast to what God commanded. Because of this, they were spared persecution.

The final church, Laodicea, was a church that literally made the Lord sick. From the outside they looked liked a great group of people. It was a church of great wealth, but inside their hearts was a great lack of spirituality. They were trusting in worldly things and not the Provider. Going through the motions, they were not on fire for God, but doing the bare minimum. They were a great social club but worthless to the kingdom.

> Which church do you identify with most? What words of warning from God speak to you the most? What words of encouragement did you need to hear?

> Just like the churches mentioned here, no church is perfect. And Jesus wants us to view our churches with an open heart rather than a critical spirit. Why do you think He cares about the health of the entire church?

God, help me to heed any warnings You send my way. I pray for my church now, that we will follow You wherever You want us to go. Amen.

NEW THINGS

What new thing do you enjoy most? Why?

New car smell

New, clean sheets

New clothes

New technology

Other: _____

We all long for new. New is often preferable to the old and worn out. New, as such, is more of a concept than an actual thing. It's a state of being.

Everything wears out—clothes, cars, shoes, minds, bodies, even universes. Science may predict the inevitable death of the universe—expansion, molecule separation, you know, the common everyday stuff we discuss around the water cooler. But God has revealed another plan.

John records his vision of the end.

> [1] Then I saw a new heaven and a new earth, for the first heaven and the first earth had passed away, and the sea no longer existed. [2] I also saw the Holy City, new Jerusalem, coming down out of heaven from God, prepared like a bride adorned for her husband. [3] Then I heard a loud voice from the throne:
> Look! God's dwelling is with humanity,
> and He will live with them.
> They will be His people,
> and God Himself will be with them
> and be their God.
> 4 He will wipe away every tear from their eyes.
> Death will no longer exist;
> grief, crying, and pain will exist no longer,
> because the previous things have passed away.
> [5] Then the One seated on the throne said, "Look! I am making everything new."
> REVELATION 21:1-5

In what area of your life would you really like to experience something new?

When was the last time you experienced tears or grief or pain? What does it mean to you to know these things will no longer exist?

Can you imagine what that is going to look like? What God makes new will never decay, never rot, never grow old, never wear out.

Jesus is preparing a place for us and when the time is right, He will bring us to where He is. Our earth and everything on it will be changed. God will walk with His people again, and we will see Him face to face.

> ² In My Father's house are many dwelling places; if not, I would
> have told you. I am going away to prepare a place for you.
> ³ If I go away and prepare a place for you, I will come back and
> receive you to Myself, so that where I am you may be also.
> JOHN 14:2-3

Question: What's the purpose for the new heaven and earth? Why is Jesus going to prepare another place? Answer: You.

He's preparing a place for you. How are you preparing for Him?

Thank You, God, for Your promise to make me new. Help me to live in Your promise now, knowing someday I will live with You forever.

VISION OF THE FUTURE

If you had the opportunity to write about an important, historical event 500 years before it happened, how would you want to reveal the information? Why?

If you have ever played "hidden treasure" with your kids, then you know a thing or two about notes and clues, maps and mystery, and the intrigue and satisfaction of a good mystery revealed. Where's the fun in hiding one note for your kids in plain site that reads, "The candy is next to the remote. Now go watch TV"? It isn't being suggested that prophecy is a game to God. But you cannot deny that God takes pleasure in revealing a good mystery in His timing, not ours.

The Book of Daniel is a narrative that tells Daniel's story. He was a prophet with a band of brothers who courageously lived for God. His book is prophetically filled with vivid dreams and visions, some of which he could not explain. Even when they were explained by angels, Daniel was troubled by them and couldn't understand.

> This is the end of the interpretation. As for me,
> Daniel, my thoughts terrified me greatly, and my face
> turned pale, but I kept the matter to myself.
> DANIEL 7:28

What interests you most about Bible prophecy? Is it difficult for you? Frightening? Exciting?

Some put an equal sign between the Books of Daniel and Revelation for several reasons: (1) Both are prophetic and revelatory in nature; (2) Both have descriptions of strange visions and dreams; and (3) Both point the reader past the present sufferings to a future where God will come and put an end to all suffering forever.

The major visions of the second half of Daniel are generally explained as events that have already happened—they were prophetic but have already come to pass. For example, Daniel's vision in chapter 7 about the four beasts represent subsequent kingdoms that rise up and conquer the others and rule over Israel. The lion represents Babylon. The bear is Media-Persia. The leopard is Greece. And the beast with 10 horns and one little horn is Rome. The fourth beast will be worse than all the others because it will rule the earth and persecute God's people for a time after which Rome's empire will end.

Another of Daniel's visions involved a war between kings of the North and kings of the South. This prophecy came to pass in startling detail in a war between the Seleucids and the Ptolemies. The warring sides fought for everything Alexander the Great left behind after his death.

The Seventy-Week Prophecy, also known as the seventy "sevens," is still prevalently discussed to this day, and for good reason. If each day in this prophecy represents one year, then you have 69 weeks, or 483 days, from the time the King of Persia granted permission for Nehemiah to rebuild the wall of Jerusalem to the time of the death of Christ. That means there is only one week left, or seven years, of Daniel's prophecy that has yet to be fulfilled. The final seven years corresponds to the tribulation in the Book of Revelation. Thus all of Daniel's prophecies have come to pass except the final prophecy—the return of Christ.

> How do you respond to such accurate prophecy that was written centuries before it happened?

Bible prophecy helps us determine whether or not God exists. But more than that, if we understand from Bible prophecy that God is true to His Word, then we can know that what God has promised to those who will listen to Him is sure and certain. God has a plan. God is true to His Word.

> How has Bible prophecy impacted how much you trust God?

God, I may not understand everything, but I trust You to bring to pass everything You have purposed. Help me to live my life expecting and attentive to Jesus' return.

JESUS, DANIEL, AND THE END

Have you ever made a statement that was totally misinterpreted? How were you able to clarify what you really meant? Or were you?

This happened to Jesus a lot. There were daily occurrences like this for the disciples as they traveled with Jesus. One time, He had been teaching in the temple complex and His disciples made a comment about the architectural beauty.

> [2] He replied to them, "Don't you see all these things? I assure you: Not one stone will be left here on another that will not be thrown down!" [3] While He was sitting on the Mount of Olives, the disciples approached Him privately and said, "Tell us, when will these things happen? And what is the sign of Your coming and of the end of the age?" [4] Then Jesus replied to them: "Watch out that no one deceives you. [5] For many will come in My name, saying, 'I am the Messiah,' and they will deceive many. [6] You are going to hear of wars and rumors of wars. See that you are not alarmed, because these things must take place, but the end is not yet. [7] For nation will rise up against nation, and kingdom against kingdom. There will be famines and earthquakes in various places. [8] All these events are the beginning of birth pains. [9] Then they will hand you over for persecution, and they will kill you. You will be hated by all nations because of My name. [10] Then many will take offense, betray one another and hate one another. [11] Many false prophets will rise up and deceive many. [12] Because lawlessness will multiply, the love of many will grow cold. [13] But the one who endures to the end will be delivered. [14] This good news of the kingdom will be proclaimed in all the world as a testimony to all nations. And then the end will come."
>
> MATTHEW 24:2-14

How do you respond to those who speak in mystery and prophecy? From this week of study, how has your desire to understand biblical prophesy changed?

Jesus then spoke of an "abomination that causes desolation" (v. 15). Daniel first spoke of this. His prophecy was that at some point the temple itself would be desecrated and sacrilegious offerings would be made. This came to pass under the rule of Antiochus IV Epiphanes. He heard that Jerusalem was in revolt and sent his armies to kill as many people as it took to reclaim the territory. The army dedicated the temple to the Greek god Zeus and forbade the Jews from performing any kind of religious ceremony. The penalty for disobedience would be death.

Jesus used this abomination that causes desolation prophecy to predict two more events. One would happen in the near future, and one would happen in the end times. The first happened when Rome (beginning under Nero) would destroy the temple and persecute Christ followers. We know this to be true. But the second prediction pointed to an event for the end times. The act of desecration wouldn't be just an event. It would be a person, standing in the Holy Place, pretending to be Christ. The abomination of desolation in the end will be a person, the Antichrist. This person will set himself up as God and will use the temple to demand worship.

> 30 Then the sign of the Son of Man will appear in the sky,
> and then all the peoples of the earth will mourn; and they
> will see the Son of Man coming on the clouds of heaven
> with power and great glory. 31 He will send out His angels
> with a loud trumpet, and they will gather His elect from
> the four winds, from one end of the sky to the other.
> MATTHEW 24:30-31

The main thrust of Jesus' message is to be prepared—He asks us all to recognize the signs and be prepared.

How can you stay on alert and be prepared for the second coming of Jesus? What do you do to keep yourself from being led astray by false teaching?

God, help me to keep my focus on You. Give me eyes to recognize false teaching and to run from it. And guide me in how I can best prepare to meet You when You return.

ALPHA AND OMEGA

What do you wish to see before the end? What does your heart long to witness?

> [12] Look! I am coming quickly, and My reward is with Me to repay each person according to what he has done. [13] I am the Alpha and the Omega, the First and the Last, the Beginning and the End.
>
> REVELATION 22:12-13

Everything that has a beginning must have an end. We began this journey with "In the beginning," when there was nothing. God created everything with a thought, a spoken word. He created mankind in His image, in His presence. But ever since Adam and Eve began the pursuit of the knowledge of good and evil, it has been the undoing of us all. Concerning a good God pursuing His people in an evil world, consider what we now know:

We know that God loves the entire world.

> God loved the world in this way: He gave His One and Only Son, so that everyone who believes in Him will not perish but have eternal life.
>
> JOHN 3:16

We know that God wishes that all would repent.

> The Lord does not delay His promise, as some understand delay, but is patient with you, not wanting any to perish but all to come to repentance.
>
> 2 PETER 3:9

We know that hell was created for Satan and the fallen angels.

> Then He will also say to those on the left, "Depart from Me, you who are cursed, into the eternal fire prepared for the Devil and his angels!"
>
> MATTHEW 25:41

We know that God wants anyone and everyone to call on His name.
¹² There is no distinction between Jew and Greek, since
the same Lord of all is rich to all who call on Him. ¹³ For
everyone who calls on the name of the Lord will be saved.
ROMANS 10:12-13

We know that Jesus leads us to God, and He is the only way.
Jesus told him, "I am the way, the truth, and the life.
No one comes to the Father except through Me."
JOHN 14:6

We know that God will never turn anyone away.
Everyone the Father gives Me will come to Me, and
the one who comes to Me I will never cast out.
JOHN 6:37

We know that God wants the gospel taken to the entire world.
This good news of the kingdom will be proclaimed in all the
world as a testimony to all nations. And then the end will come.
MATTHEW 24:14

What else is there to know? What else is there to do? Love God, love others, make
disciples, and be ready.

Who do you need to love to Christ?

Who do you need to invest in spiritually?

How can you be ready?

---

*God, thank You for Your promises. I look forward to the day when You defeat evil
and the Evil One once and for all. Lord Jesus, come quickly. Amen.*

LEADER GUIDE

We're glad you've chosen to take your small group through *Fast Track*. It is our prayer that this study will guide your group members into a better understanding of God's Word by being able to track along with main characters, major events, and thematic movements of Scripture. Before you get started, here is some helpful information about the different elements you'll encounter within the study as well as the resources you will find on the following pages.

WEEK INTRODUCTION: Each session begins with a narrative overview of the weekly content. This material is designed to help you introduce the topic of study. You will want to read this before your group meets so that you'll better understand the context for your time together. For weeks 2-8 suggest that group members read this before you meet.

BACK TRACK: This time is designed to provide group members with an opportunity to talk about what God has been revealing to them or what internal dialogue or conclusions have resulted from their Personal Track time during the past week.

FRAMING THE STORY: Your actual group time will most likely begin here with an icebreaker that is designed to help you ease into the study and get everyone talking. These questions are intended to be nonthreatening to group members so that a pattern of participation can be established early on.

VIDEO TRACK: The first page of this section provides group members with a tic-tac-toe grid where they can draw the icons for each week as they watch Chad draw them in the video. The second page provides some of the key points from Chad's teaching as well as a notes area where group members can jot down important points from Chad's message that were particularly meaningful to them.

GROUP TRACK: This portion of your weekly group meeting will guide group members to examine passages that reinforce what Chad is teaching in his video message. Each question is designed to lead the group deeper into the truth of the Scriptures they are studying as well as to give them an opportunity to explore some of the major events, circumstances, or biblical figures identified in their study that week.

NOTE: The Group Track portion of your meeting each week is built around four types of questions. You may find it helpful to familiarize yourself with these:

- **Observation—What is this passage telling us?**
  Observation questions help group members identify what the biblical text is saying. Asking this type of question usually causes members to look back at the passage in order to discover the answer.

- **Interpretation—What does the passage mean?**
  The purpose of an interpretation question is to discover what the text means. While each passage has many applications, it only has one interpretation. These questions cause the group to wrestle with the meaning of a verse or passage.

- **Application—Now that I know what I know, what will I do to integrate this truth into my life?**
  Application questions help group members see how they can act on the principle they discovered in the passage. Good application questions will help people to think, *What should I do about this?* We are bringing the truth back into our culture/context and applying it here and now.

- **Self-Revelation—How am I doing in light of the truth unveiled?**
  Self-revelation questions require the reader to assess personal progress in applying the truth. This is the most intimately revealing question to ask. We are identifying to what degree we are living the truth.

WRAP: During this portion of your small-group time you will watch a short closing video message from Chad and spend a few minutes discussing what he shares, as well as wrapping up your meeting for the week. You will also use this time to close the group in prayer, using the prayer provided in each session as your guide.

PERSONAL TRACK: There are five devotionals following each small-group session. These will give group members an opportunity to take what they've learned during the session and continue the conversation in private devotional settings with God.

Session 1
TRUST ME

SESSION INTRODUCTION

Welcome group members to the study and make sure everyone has a workbook. You may want to have a marker and name tags on hand (just for the first week), especially if it's a group that's new to each other. Consider jumping to the Back Track section first this week and then introducing the topic for Session 1.

BACK TRACK

In weeks 2-8 this time will be used to talk about what God has been revealing to group members or what conclusions or internal dialogue have resulted from their Personal Track time during the week. But for the first session, take a few moments for the group to share any personal goals they have for this study. Be ready to share your own goals to get the conversation going.

FRAMING THE STORY

Give everyone an opportunity to answer the question that introduces this week's topic—trusting God. The icebreaker will get the group thinking about the topic in general terms. Continue to encourage all group members to share during this time. Some members will be more comfortable speaking aloud than others. Just remember that the objective is to give everyone the opportunity to get involved.

VIDEO TRACK

Each of Chad's video messages contains three segments: an opening illustration, the main teaching time, and a conclusion. For the Video Track time, play the first two segments and then stop the video. When you get to the wrap portion of your group time, play the concluding segment.

Play the video for Session 1 (30:00). Encourage group members to follow along with Chad using the tic-tac-toe grid provided in their workbook. They can take additional notes on the facing page when they hear something that resonates with them.

GROUP TRACK

After the group has watched the video, you will lead them right into the small-group discussion time. Before your meeting, check the Leader Helps on the DVD-ROM in your leader kit for additional group discussion guidance. We have taken each question from the Group Track time and provided an explanation for why it is included as well as examples of possible responses.

In this session you will examine in more detail obstacles that contribute to us not trusting God, as well as the difference in trusting God with the big things and trusting Him with the small things.

Wrap: Show the closing segment of Chad's teaching video (3:30) and then spend a few minutes processing what he said. Summarize the concluding remarks to wrap up your group session and lead into the closing prayer.

Prayer: After the Wrap, you will want to conclude your group time in prayer. Use the prayer provided at the bottom of the Wrap section to guide your thoughts. For the first week, you should be the one to pray aloud. In the coming weeks, when your group gets more comfortable, consider asking volunteers to pray.

PERSONAL TRACK

Encourage group members to complete all five Personal Track devotionals before your next group meeting. Remind them that they will have a chance to talk about what God has shown them through their time with Him.

Share that next week you will be looking at Exodus through 1 Samuel and talking about what it means to not give up on God.

Session 2
DON'T GIVE UP

SESSION INTRODUCTION

Welcome group members back. Use the narrative overview to help you introduce the topic of study for Session 2. Make sure you read this before your group meets so that you'll better understand the topic and context for your time together.

BACK TRACK

Before you move forward, take a moment to review last week. Talk about things that may have provoked new thoughts about trusting God as well as changes group members feel they need to make to move forward in trusting Him more and more.

FRAMING THE STORY

Give everyone an opportunity to answer the question. Continue to encourage all group members to share during this time.

VIDEO TRACK

Each of Chad's video messages contains three segments: an opening illustration, the main teaching time, and a conclusion. For the Video Track time, play the first two segments and then stop the video. When you get to the wrap portion of your group time, play the concluding segment.

Play the video for Session 2 (27:00). Encourage group members to follow along with Chad using the tic-tac-toe grid provided in their workbook. They can take additional notes on the facing page when they hear something that resonates with them.

GROUP TRACK

After the group has watched the video, you will lead them right into the small-group discussion time. Before your meeting, check the Leader Helps on the DVD-ROM in your leader kit for additional group discussion guidance.

In this session you will talk about God's expectations for us to not give up on Him, the importance of seeing ourselves the way He sees us, and what it means to have faith the size of a mustard seed.

Wrap: Show the closing segment of Chad's teaching video (5:00) and then spend a few minutes processing what he said. Summarize the concluding remarks to wrap up your group session and lead into the closing prayer.

Prayer: After the Wrap, you will want to conclude your group time in prayer. Use the prayer provided at the bottom of the Wrap section to guide your thoughts. This week you may consider asking a volunteer to lead the prayer. If you lead the prayer, ask God to give each person the strength he or she needs to keep going with Him and never give up.

PERSONAL TRACK

Encourage group members to complete all five Personal Track devotionals before your next group meeting. Remind them that they will have a chance to talk about what God has shown them through their time with Him.

Share that next week you will be looking at 1 Samuel through 1 Kings and talking about what happens when we stop running and return to God.

Session 3
STOP RUNNING AND RETURN TO ME

SESSION INTRODUCTION

Welcome group members back. Use the narrative overview to help you introduce the topic of study for Session 3. As always, make sure you read this before your group meets so that you'll better understand the topic and context for your time together.

BACK TRACK

Start your small-group session by looking back at last week. The Personal Track devotionals focused on different aspects of never giving up. Encourage group members to speak up about how God has inspired or challenged them to engage their faith or move past self-doubt. Use this time to encourage your group with words of affirmation and positive feedback.

FRAMING THE STORY

Give everyone an opportunity to answer the question. This activity may conjure up visual images, thoughts, or memories about running away from home—from their own lives or the lives of people they know. Continue to encourage all group members to share during this time.

VIDEO TRACK

Play the video for Session 3 (28:00). Encourage group members to follow along with Chad using the tic-tac-toe grid provided in their workbook. They can take additional notes on the facing page when they hear something that resonates with them.

GROUP TRACK

After the group has watched the video, you will lead them right into the small-group discussion time. Before your meeting, check the Leader Helps on the DVD-ROM in your leader kit for additional group discussion guidance.

In this session you will discuss possible obstacles that try to keep us from following God and how we can best ignore distractions and keep our eyes on Him.

Wrap: Show the closing segment of Chad's teaching video (4:30) and then spend a few minutes processing what he said. Summarize the concluding remarks to wrap up your group session and lead into the closing prayer.

Prayer: After the Wrap, you will want to conclude your group time in prayer. Use the prayer provided at the bottom of the Wrap section to guide your thoughts. Close the group in prayer, asking God to help you stop running and find your way back to Him.

PERSONAL TRACK

Encourage group members to complete all five Personal Track devotionals before your next group meeting. Remind them that they will have a chance to talk about what God has shown them through their time with Him.

Share that next week you will be looking at 2 Kings through Malachi and talking about what it means to keep God first.

Session 4
KEEP GOD FIRST

SESSION INTRODUCTION

Welcome group members back. Use the narrative overview to help you introduce the topic of study for Session 4. Make sure you read this before your group meets so that you'll better understand the topic and context for your time together.

BACK TRACK

Start the session off by looking back at the past week. This week group members will have the opportunity to share how God has used difficult times to teach them how to run back to Him.

FRAMING THE STORY

Give everyone an opportunity to answer the question here. This activity offers a chance for a little healthy, playful debate—depending on how strongly group members feel about their own opinion. This should be a non-threatening activity. Have fun with it.

VIDEO TRACK

Play the video for Session 4 (27:30). Encourage group members to follow along with Chad using the tic-tac-toe grid provided in their workbook. They can take additional notes on the facing page when they hear something that resonates with them.

GROUP TRACK

After the group has watched the video, you will lead them right into the small-group discussion time. Before your meeting, check the Leader Helps on the DVD-ROM in your leader kit for additional group discussion guidance.

In this session you will look more closely at the story of Jonah and the problems in his life that kept him from putting God first. And on a more personal note you will talk about times when you have been upset about something God asked you to do.

Wrap: Show the closing segment of Chad's teaching video (5:00) and then spend a few minutes processing what he said. Summarize the concluding remarks to wrap up your group session and lead into the closing prayer.

Prayer: After the Wrap, conclude your group time in prayer. Use the prayer provided at the bottom of the Wrap section to guide your thoughts. Ask for a volunteer to start the prayer. As the leader, close the prayer time by asking God to help you all act in ways that show you are keeping Him first.

PERSONAL TRACK

Encourage group members to complete all five Personal Track devotionals before your next group meeting. Remind them that they will have a chance to talk about what God has shown them through their time with Him.

Share that next week you will be covering Job, Ruth, Lamentations, and Psalms. You will examine the lives of believers who continued to engage God even in the midst of their doubt.

Session 5
FACING ADVERSITY

SESSION INTRODUCTION

Welcome group members back. Use the narrative overview to help you introduce the topic of study for Session 5. Make sure you read this before your group meets so that you'll better understand the topic and context for your time together.

BACK TRACK

Before you move forward, take a moment to review last week. Talk with group members about what God has been teaching them related to keeping Him first, how He has gotten their attention, and how they see God working and accomplishing His purposes in their lives.

FRAMING THE STORY

Give everyone an opportunity to answer the question. This activity invokes the movie lover in all of us. Encourage all group members to share during this time.

VIDEO TRACK

Play the video for Session 5 (32:00). Encourage group members to follow along with Chad using the tic-tac-toe grid provided in their workbook. They can take additional notes on the facing page when they hear something that resonates with them.

GROUP TRACK

After the group has watched the video, lead them right into the small-group discussion time. Before your meeting, check the Leader Helps on the DVD-ROM in your leader kit for additional group discussion guidance.

In this session you will talk about circumstances that cause you to doubt, questions you ask God, and what it means to truly know God.

Wrap: Show the closing segment of Chad's teaching video (5:00) and then spend a few minutes processing what he said. Summarize the concluding remarks to wrap up your group session and lead into the closing prayer.

Prayer: After the Wrap, you will want to conclude your group time in prayer. Use the prayer provided at the bottom of the Wrap section to guide your thoughts. Ask for a volunteer to open your prayer time and open the floor for anyone to pray who would like to. Close the prayer time, asking God to help you not focus on the circumstances around you, but on His strength instead.

PERSONAL TRACK

Encourage group members to complete all five Personal Track devotionals before your next group meeting. Remind them that they will have a chance to talk about what God has shown them through their time with Him.

Share that next week you will be covering Matthew through John and talking about God's greatest gift—Jesus Christ.

Session 6
GOD'S GREATEST GIFT

SESSION INTRODUCTION

Welcome group members back. Use the narrative overview to help you introduce the topic of study for Session 6. Make sure you read this before your group meets so that you'll better understand the topic and context for your time together.

BACK TRACK

Before you move forward, take a moment to review the past week. The Personal Track devotionals centered around different aspects of doubting God during the bad times. Ask your group what healthy ways they have found to lament and vent when things go wrong. Also take a few minutes to talk about ways they have experienced their faith increasing and their doubt decreasing.

FRAMING THE STORY

Take turns answering the questions. They are so simple, everyone should be able to answer: "What's a favorite gift you received?" and "What's a favorite gift you gave?"

VIDEO TRACK

Play the video for Session 6 (33:00). Encourage group members to follow along with Chad using the tic-tac-toe grid provided in their workbook. They can take additional notes on the facing page when they hear something that resonates with them.

GROUP TRACK

After the group has watched the video, lead them right into the small-group discussion time. Before your meeting, check the Leader Helps on the DVD-ROM in your leader kit for additional group discussion guidance.

In this session you will talk about the transforming power of Jesus Christ as well as who you say He is.

Be Aware: This session may prompt members to ask questions if they are unsure of their relationship with the Lord. If you need to show someone how to make a commitment to Christ after your meeting, show them The Gift of Jesus Christ on page 186 and lead them through the Scriptures listed there.

Wrap: Show the closing segment of Chad's teaching video (5:00) and then spend a few minutes processing what he said. Summarize the concluding remarks to wrap up your group session and lead into the closing prayer.

Prayer: After the Wrap, conclude your group time in prayer. Use the prayer provided at the bottom of the Wrap section to guide your thoughts. Spend time thanking God for His Son. Give group members an opportunity to pray and thank God for all the gifts He has given them.

PERSONAL TRACK

Encourage group members to complete all five Personal Track devotionals before your next group meeting. Remind them that they will have a chance to talk about what God has shown them through their time with Him.

Share that next week you will be covering Acts through Thessalonians and talking about our call to participate with God as His ambassadors to a broken world.

Session 7
A NEW MISSION

SESSION INTRODUCTION

Welcome group members back. Use the narrative overview to help you introduce the topic of study for Session 7. Make sure you read this before your group meets so that you'll better understand the topic and context for your time together.

BACK TRACK

Before you move forward, take a moment to review last week. The Personal Track devotionals centered on the freedom we have in Christ. Encourage your group members to share how they operate in the freedom of Jesus Christ.

FRAMING THE STORY

Take turns answering the question. This activity turns the discussion toward adventure. Choose which real-life adventure you would most like to participate in. Encourage group members to dream big!

VIDEO TRACK

Play the video for Session 7 (29:00). Encourage group members to follow along with Chad using the tic-tac-toe grid provided in their workbook. They can take additional notes on the facing page when they hear something that resonates with them.

GROUP TRACK

After the group has watched the video, lead them right into the small-group discussion time. Before your meeting, check the Leader Helps on the DVD-ROM in your leader kit for additional group discussion guidance.

In this session you will discuss our mission with God here on earth. Group members will also have an opportunity to talk about what big things they would like to accomplish with God if money was not an issue.

Wrap: Show the closing segment of Chad's teaching video (5:00) and then spend a few minutes processing what he said. Summarize the concluding remarks to wrap up your group session and lead into the closing prayer.

Prayer: After the Wrap, you will want to conclude your group time in prayer. Use the prayer provided at the bottom of the Wrap section to guide your thoughts. Have someone close the group in prayer or conclude yourself. If you lead the prayer, ask God to make known His mission and task to each of your group members.

PERSONAL TRACK

Encourage group members to complete all five Personal Track devotionals before your next group meeting. Remind them that they will have a chance to talk about what God has shown them through their time with Him.

Share that next week you will be covering Revelation, Daniel, and Matthew 24 and talking about prophesies fulfilled as well as those yet to be fulfilled. You'll also talk about what is next for your group when you complete your study of *Fast Track*, so encourage group members to think about what they would like to see happen.

Session 8
NEVER GIVE UP

SESSION INTRODUCTION

Welcome group members back for your last session of *Fast Track*. Use the narrative overview to help you introduce the topic of study for Session 8. Make sure you read this before your group meets so that you'll better understand the topic and context for your time together.

BACK TRACK

Before you move forward, take a moment to review the previous week. Let group members use this time to share what the Holy Spirit is teaching them about being on mission and how they are loving and investing in others.

FRAMING THE STORY

Give everyone an opportunity to answer the questions. These activities draw attention to how secular stories and movies have depicted the future as well as what group members think our world may look like in 50 or 100 years if Jesus doesn't come back first.

VIDEO TRACK

Note: In this video message, Chad teaches one particular eschatological position. We realize there are many positions on the subject of end times and members of your group may have differing views. Please keep this in mind and consider pointing this out to your group before you begin the video portion of your small-group time.

Play the video for Session 8 (31:00). Encourage group members to follow along with Chad using the tic-tac-toe grid provided in their workbook. They can take additional notes on the facing page when they hear something that resonates with them.

GROUP TRACK

After the group has watched the video, lead them right into the small-group discussion time. Before your meeting, check the Leader Helps on the DVD-ROM in your leader kit for additional group discussion guidance.

In this session you will talk in practical terms about what it means to be ready for Jesus' return even if we don't know when He is coming.

Wrap: Show the closing segment of Chad's teaching video (5:00) and then spend a few minutes processing what he said. Chad uses this final video segment in a powerful way. Encourage your group members to fully engage in this worshipful experience. Also allow time to complete the activity together and use this as an opportunity to acknowledge the impact this study has had on you.

Prayer: After the Wrap, you will want to conclude your group time in prayer. Use the prayer provided at the bottom of the Wrap section to guide your thoughts. Invite group members to pray aloud in closing. Thank God for this eight-week journey you have just completed together. When all have prayed who wish to, close the prayer by asking God to help you put into practice all you have learned. Ask Him to use your group members to love and lead others to Jesus Christ.

PERSONAL TRACK

Encourage group members to complete all five Personal Track devotionals even though you won't come together again as a group to discuss them. Suggest that they take some extra time to reflect on what they have learned through this study of *Fast Track* and where the Lord may be leading them next.

Before everyone gets away, talk about what's next for your group. If you want to stay together and do another study, check out *lifeway.com/smallgroups* for options. You might also consider splitting into two groups to make room for new members.

THE GIFT OF JESUS CHRIST

Jesus is the bold collision between the Divine One—God—and the desperate ones—us. He is great enough to be the Savior of the world but personal enough to be our Lord and Savior.

But according to Jesus, there is something that must happen inside of us if we are to fully embrace who He is. That "something" is so drastic, so complete, so life-changing that the only way to describe it is through the process of new birth. It is only after that new birth that we can truly walk in relationship with Jesus.

The fact is that we need to be changed. It is not enough for us to believe there is a God, pray regularly, attend church, or just be a spiritual person. That does not take care of what our real issue is. The real issue is sin—not just the little lies we tell or the extra income we don't report to the IRS, but the fact that our nature, our very identity, is corrupted with rebellion against God. That's why we need a complete change. It is because our corruption runs so deep that we need to be a whole new person.

This is what Jesus came to offer. According to the Bible, this sin problem is universal in scope, and the just punishment for it is being separated from God for all time (Romans 6:23). But Jesus' death on the cross is an offer to take care of that. Jesus took that punishment on our behalf. But just as He suffered for us, He offers us a chance to get His righteous nature, to be born again (2 Corinthians 5:21).

This does not happen by our good works. It can't be manufactured, earned, or bought. This new birth comes through faith, for as Jesus told Nicodemus, "everyone who believes in [the Son of God] will not perish but have eternal life" (John 3:16).

Ready to be something different than you are? How about a child of God? The offer is there. Why don't you take the chance today and ask your small-group leader how to begin?

FAST TRACK FAMILY OF RESOURCES

Fast Track for Adults

Member Workbook (Item 005558732)

Leader Kit (**Item** 005558795) includes:

- One *Fast Track Member Workbook*
- Two DVDs containing:
  - eight 30- to 35-minute video messages from Chad Hovind (also available as downloads at *lifeway.com/fasttrack*)
  - a PDF version of the small-group discussion questions including an explanation for each as well as examples of possible responses when applicable
  - a PDF of sermon outlines for each session
  - an electronic version of the *Fast Track Story of the Bible* booklet. This booklet is an eight-chapter summary of Genesis to Revelation that can be read straight through, integrated into the group experience by the leader, or used by group members to accompany their study a chapter at a time. Leaders have permission to make copies as needed or to send to each group member.
  - Four audio CDs of Chad's eight video messages (Also sold separately—Item 005613353. Or available as downloads at *lifeway.com/fasttrack*.)

ALSO AVAILABLE:

Fast Track for Students

In eight weeks, Chad Hovind will lead students through the major themes, characters, and events in a unique style that will help them remember and also be able to share the story in ways they haven't seen before.

Student Book (Item 005558761)

Leader Guide (Item 005558762)

Leader Kit (Item 005558763)

Fast Track for Kids

Takes kids on a fast-track trip through the Bible—Genesis to Revelation—in eight sessions. Leaders will tell, act out, and draw pictures related to the Bible stories, helping kids connect the major people and events of the Bible to Jesus.

Activity Book (Item 005557463)

Leader Guide (Item 005557462)

ICONS FROM KID'S EDITION

Session 1

Session 2

Session 3

Session 4

Session 5

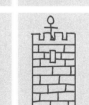 

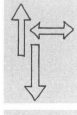 

Session 6

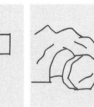 

Session 7

  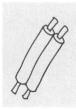

Session 8

DO YOU GO WHEREVER HE LEADS YOU?

Are you a follower of Christ? Are you sure? When Jesus says, "Come, follow Me," it is not an invitation to say a prayer. It is a summons to lose our lives. But have we? In this much-anticipated follow-up to *Radical*, David Platt continues to challenge cultural Christianity. And it just might challenge you and your entire church. So get with your group. Watch Platt on video. Take some time to retreat, reflect, and genuinely respond to Jesus' invitation, "Follow Me."

lifeway.com/followme | 800.458.2772 | LifeWay Christian Stores

GROUP DIRECTORY

Pass your books around and ask your group members to fill in their names and contact information in each other's books.

Name: _____ Name: _____
Phone: _____ Phone: _____
Email: _____ Email: _____
Social Network(s): _____ Social Network(s): _____

Name: _____ Name: _____
Phone: _____ Phone: _____
Email: _____ Email: _____
Social Network(s): _____ Social Network(s): _____

Name: _____ Name: _____
Phone: _____ Phone: _____
Email: _____ Email: _____
Social Network(s): _____ Social Network(s): _____

Name: _____ Name: _____
Phone: _____ Phone: _____
Email: _____ Email: _____
Social Network(s): _____ Social Network(s): _____

Name: _____ Name: _____
Phone: _____ Phone: _____
Email: _____ Email: _____
Social Network(s): _____ Social Network(s): _____

Name: _____ Name: _____
Phone: _____ Phone: _____
Email: _____ Email: _____
Social Network(s): _____ Social Network(s): _____

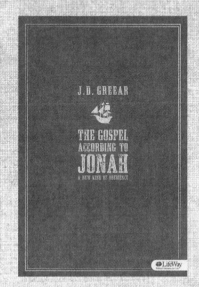